AF377697

Certification Manual

LEAN SIX SIGMA MANAGEMENT

Collection: GESTIONA
Publishing director: David Soler

LEAN SIX SIGMA MANAGEMENT. CERTIFICATION MANUAL
1st Edition, 2021

© 2021, Luis Vicente Socconini Pérez Gómez
© of this Edition: ICG Marge, SL

Publisher: Marge Books
València, 558 – 08026 Barcelona
Tel. 931 429 486 – marge@margebooks.com
www.margebooks.com

Edition coordination: Karina Ahumada Serrano
Edition: Mercedes Lara
Printed by: Safekat, SL (Madrid)

Paper Edition ISBN: 978-84-19109-01-9
Digital Edition ISBN: 978-84-19109-02-6
Legal Deposit:

All rights reserved. No part of this publication, including the cover design, may be reproduced, stored, transmitted, distributed, used, publicly announced or transformed in any form or by any means (electronic, chemical, mechanical, optical, photocopying, recording or otherwise) without the prior written permission of the publisher, excluding exceptions established by law. Refer to Cedro (Centro Español de Derechos Reprográficos, www.conlicencia.com) if you should need to photo-copy, scan or make digital copies of any part of this book.

The paper used in this books has not been bleached with elemental chlorine (CI_2).

The author

ABOUT LUIS SOCCONINI

He holds a bachelor's degree in Industrial Engineering and a master's degree in Quality and Productivity from Monterrey Tec. He is also a Master Black Belt in Lean Six Sigma and a distinguished professor at several prestigious universities in Mexico.

Luis is certified in Strategic Management by Stanford University, in Leading Product Innovation by Harvard University, and in Industry 4.0 by MIT.

He has worked as a business consultant for the Wharton Business School in Pennsylvania, as a process engineer for Grolsch Brewery in the Netherlands, and as a manufacturing engineer at IBM.

As director of Lean Six Sigma Institute, Luis develops high-impact projects for companies such as Abbott Laboratories, Kraft Heinz, Coca-Cola, BMW, Bimbo, and Fender – to name a few. He has a broad base of experience and is continually developing productivity applications in diverse industries such as construction, mining, agriculture, government, energy, service, and more.

Luis is the author of **Lean Six Sigma Green Belt, Certification Manual, Lean Company, Lean Manufacturing, The Process of the 5's in Action,** as well as co-author of **Lean Six Sigma Management System** and **Lean Energy 4.0.**

SOCCONINI

www.socconini.com

Index

Preface

Dear Reader,

I warmly welcome you on this journey to obtain the **Lean Six Sigma Management Certification** and I wish to congratulate you because having this certification manual in your hands means that you seek to contribute to social development through the improvement of people, processes, and organizations – which ultimately leads to the well-being of our communities.

This certification manual is born from the need to share what we at Lean Six Sigma Institute (LSSI) teach people who participate in organizational processes – including managers, business owners, government officials, engineers, operators, and students. All of them receive training to transform today's key processes and design the organizations of the future.

At first, this manual was part of the material delivered to LSSI course participants across the world. Until one day, our regional Director in Spain suggested that our manuals could also be distributed in bookstores – allowing anyone to access the knowledge that is revolutionizing business thinking and the way organizations work today. We know that as long as people are trained and – above all – committed to a new spectrum of design and improvement possibilities, organizations will grow stronger as they face the new challenges posed by the ever-changing world we live in.

In this manual you will find a particularly useful toolbox that will help you successfully develop and continuously improve organizational activities. This toolbox is the result of decades of best practices proven to help organizations maximize value and achieve their goals.

You will find management tools that leaders must understand and implement in order to plan and execute strategies, analyze results, design organizational structures, nourish new talent, and develop a new financial thinking that accurately reflects real costs.

The work philosophy, tools, and methodologies explained in this manual will allow you to easily understand how the organizations of the future should be run — and will therefore enable you to become an agent of change and to produce positive, impactful results.

The goal of this certification manual is to help you understand and implement simple yet practical tools that you can also teach your colleagues and use to develop new ways of working — thus continuously adapting to complex, changing business environments.

In this world, improvement is optional — but progress is up to you. I appreciate your trust and confidence in giving us the opportunity to provide you with high-quality, widely tested material and I thank you for granting us the responsibility to guide you on this continuous improvement journey that starts but never finishes.

LUIS SOCCONINI
Founder and Director of Lean Six Sigma Institute

LSSI
LEAN SIX SIGMA INSTITUTE

Certification Manual

LEAN SIX SIGMA MANAGEMENT

Introduction to Lean Six Sigma

When the winds of change blow, some people build walls and others build windmills. Chinese Proverb

Learning objectives

1. Understand the fundamentals of Lean and Six Sigma.
2. Understand the importance of improving productivity by eliminating waste and variability.
3. Learn how to successfully implement and manage Lean Six Sigma philosophy, tools, and methodologies.
4. Develop a leadership mindset and become a change agent in establishing the structure needed to achieve impactful results.

Content

> Background
> Business Development Model
> What is Lean & Six Sigma?
> Benefits
> Implementation Process
> Change Management
> Structure and Roles
> Leadership

Background

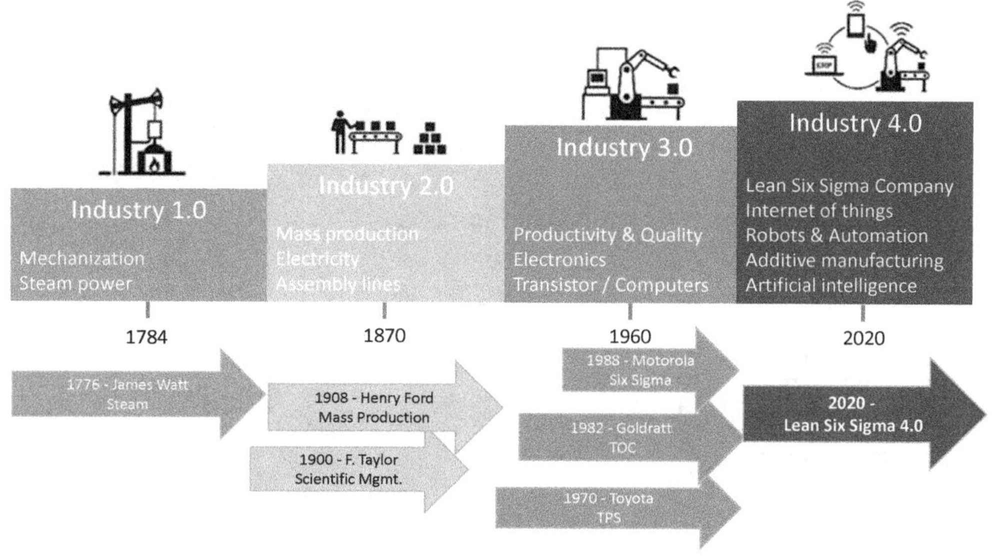

- Many companies continue to encounter:
  - Slow delivery of products or services
  - Constant customer complaints
  - Inconsistent quality
  - Poor customer service
  - High costs and prices
  - Poor internal communication

These companies are destined to vanish!

"It's not the big that eat the small...it's the fast that eat the slow."
Jason Jennins

Industry 4.0 elements

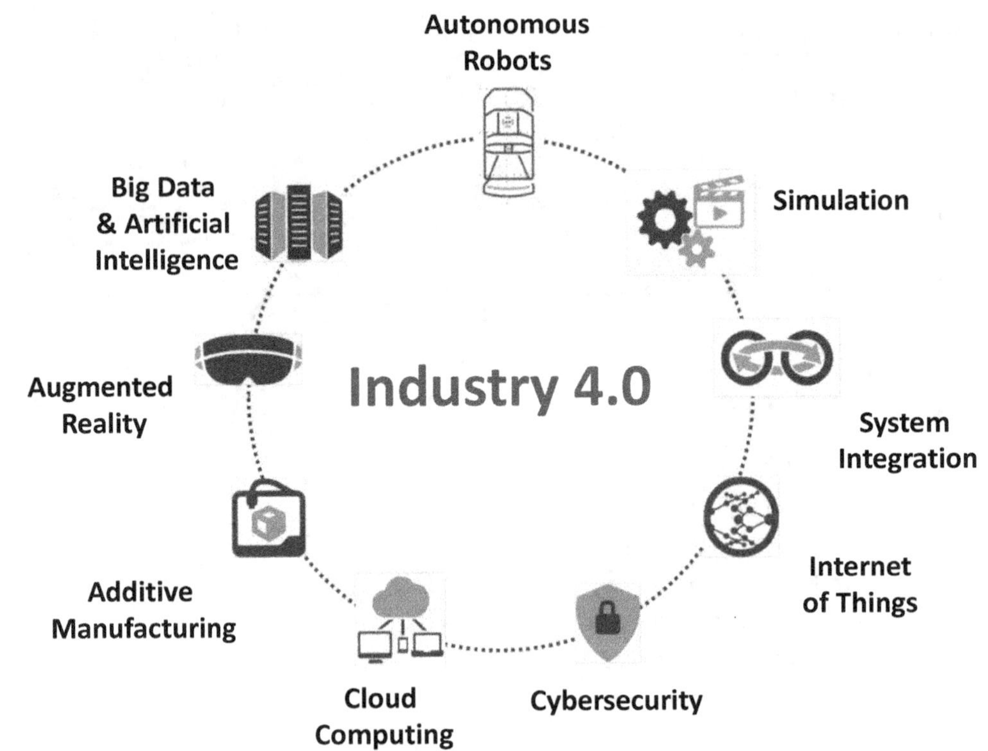

LSSI
LEAN SIX SIGMA INSTITUTE

Which model represents your business?

Traditional Thinking

Cost + Profit = Price

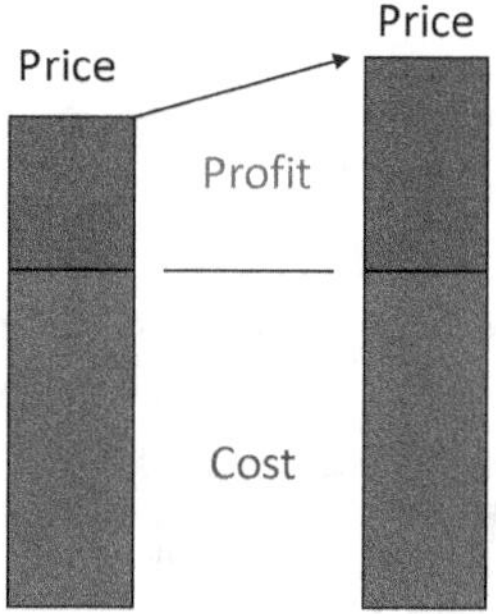

Lean Six Sigma Thinking

Price (fixed) − Cost = Profit

First level   **Second level**   **Third level**

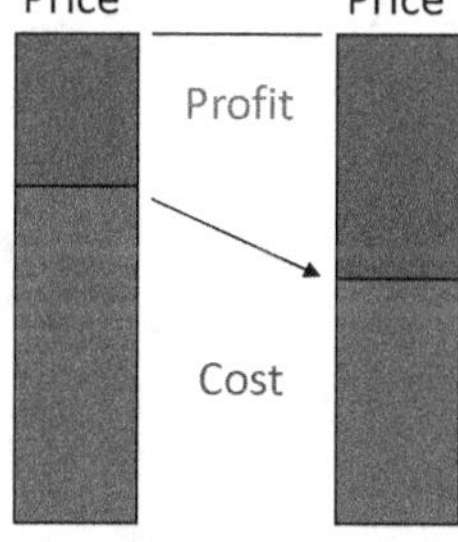

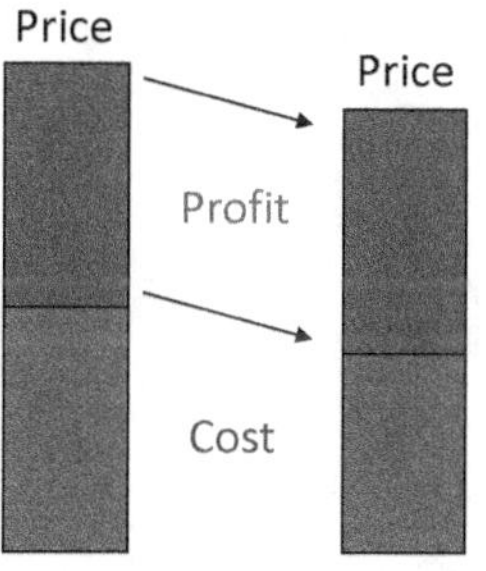

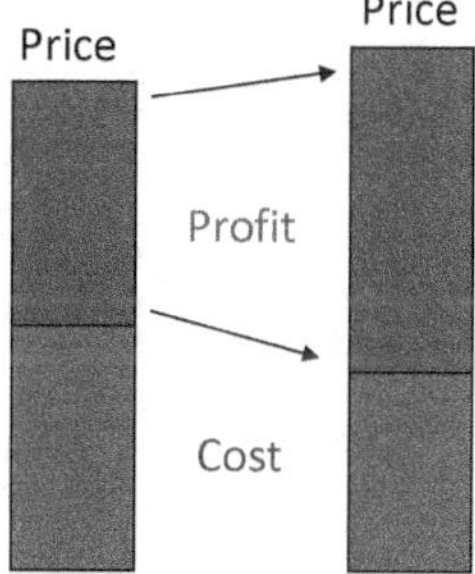

Maintain the price without sacrificing profit   Lower price without sacrificing profit   Increase price and increase profit

The key to increasing profits:
reduced costs & increased revenues

Productivity and its limitations

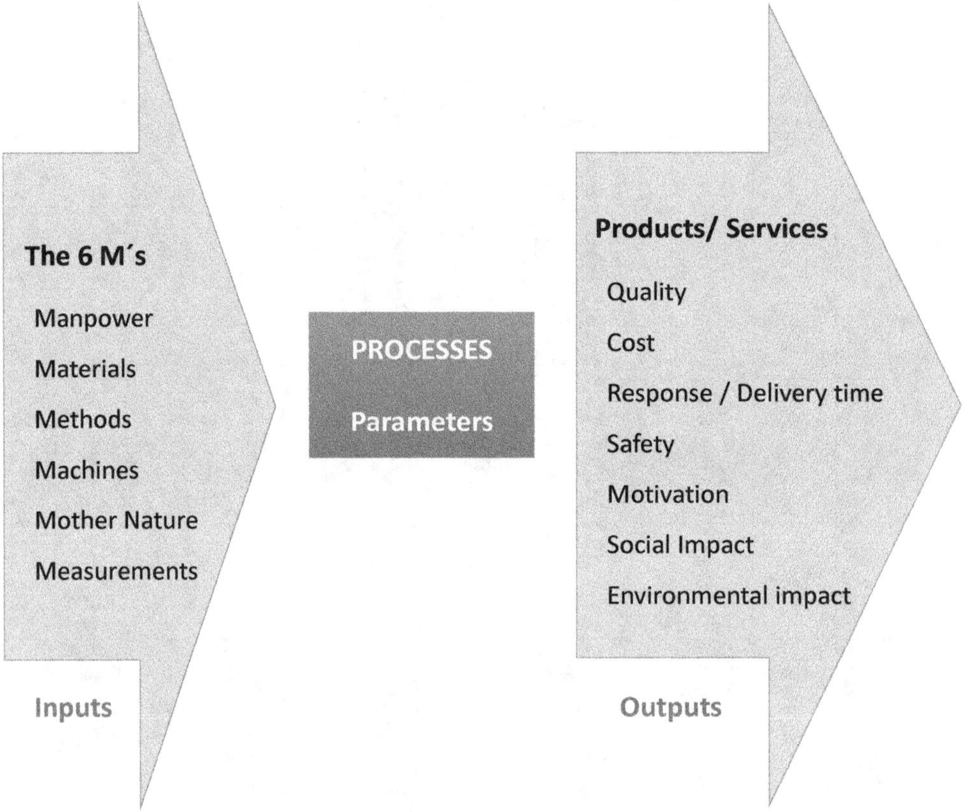

The 6 M´s

Manpower

Materials

Methods

Machines

Mother Nature

Measurements

Inputs

PROCESSES

Parameters

Products/ Services

Quality

Cost

Response / Delivery time

Safety

Motivation

Social Impact

Environmental impact

Outputs

$$\textbf{Productivity} \ = \ \frac{\text{Outputs}}{\text{Inputs}} \qquad \frac{10{,}000}{\$10{,}000} \qquad \frac{10{,}000}{\$5{,}000}$$

LSSI
LEAN SIX SIGMA INSTITUTE

Methods to increase productivity

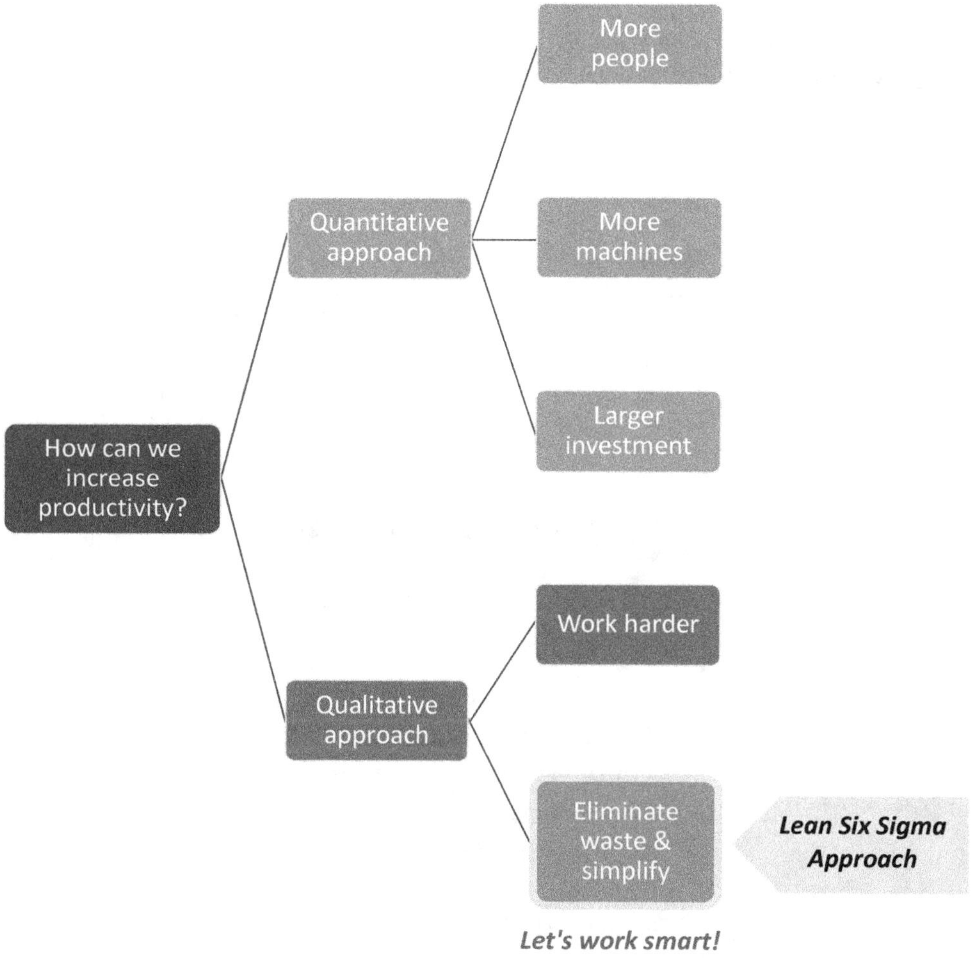

Limitations to Productivity

Muri Overburden

- Overbearing Tasks
- Work related stress
- High-Risk Tasks

Mura Variability

Total Variability
- The variation that results from all process inputs

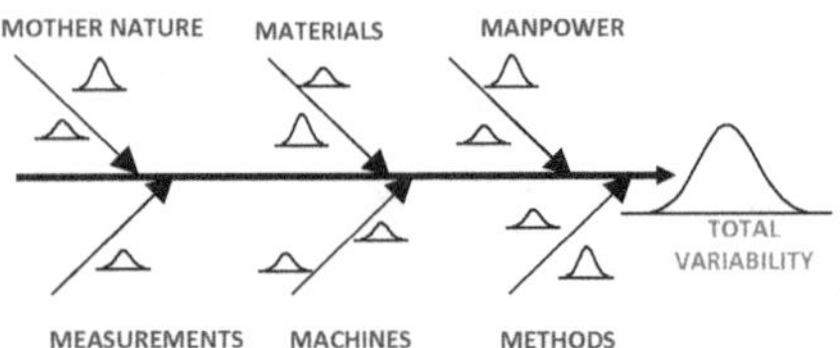

Muda Waste

- Overproduction
- Excess inventory
- Defects and Rework
- Unnecessary movements
- Overprocessing
- Waiting and Searching
- Transport
- Waste of energy
- Non-utilized talent
- Contamination / Pollution

LSSI
LEAN SIX SIGMA INSTITUTE

Lean Six Sigma reduces non-value adding time

Eliminate overload, variation, and waste

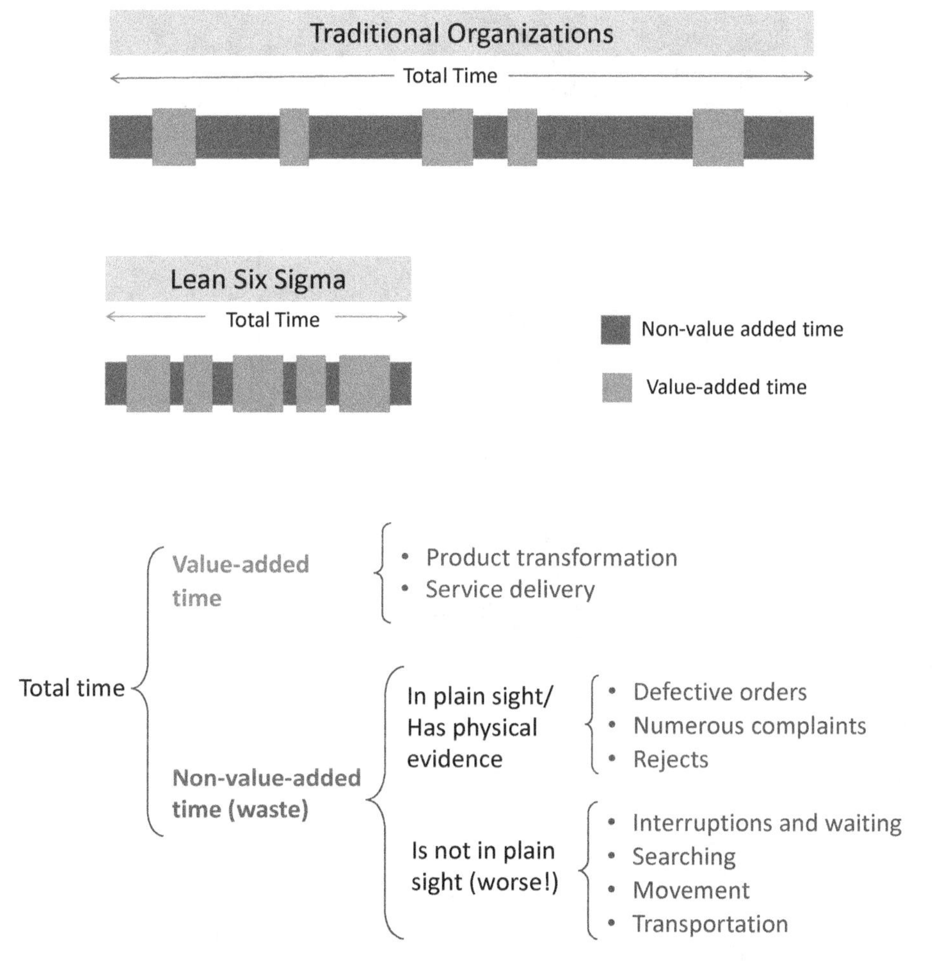

Reduce: Time, Costs, Defects, Inventory, Space, Waste.

Increase: Productivity, Customer Satisfaction, Quality, Cash Flow.

Business Development Model

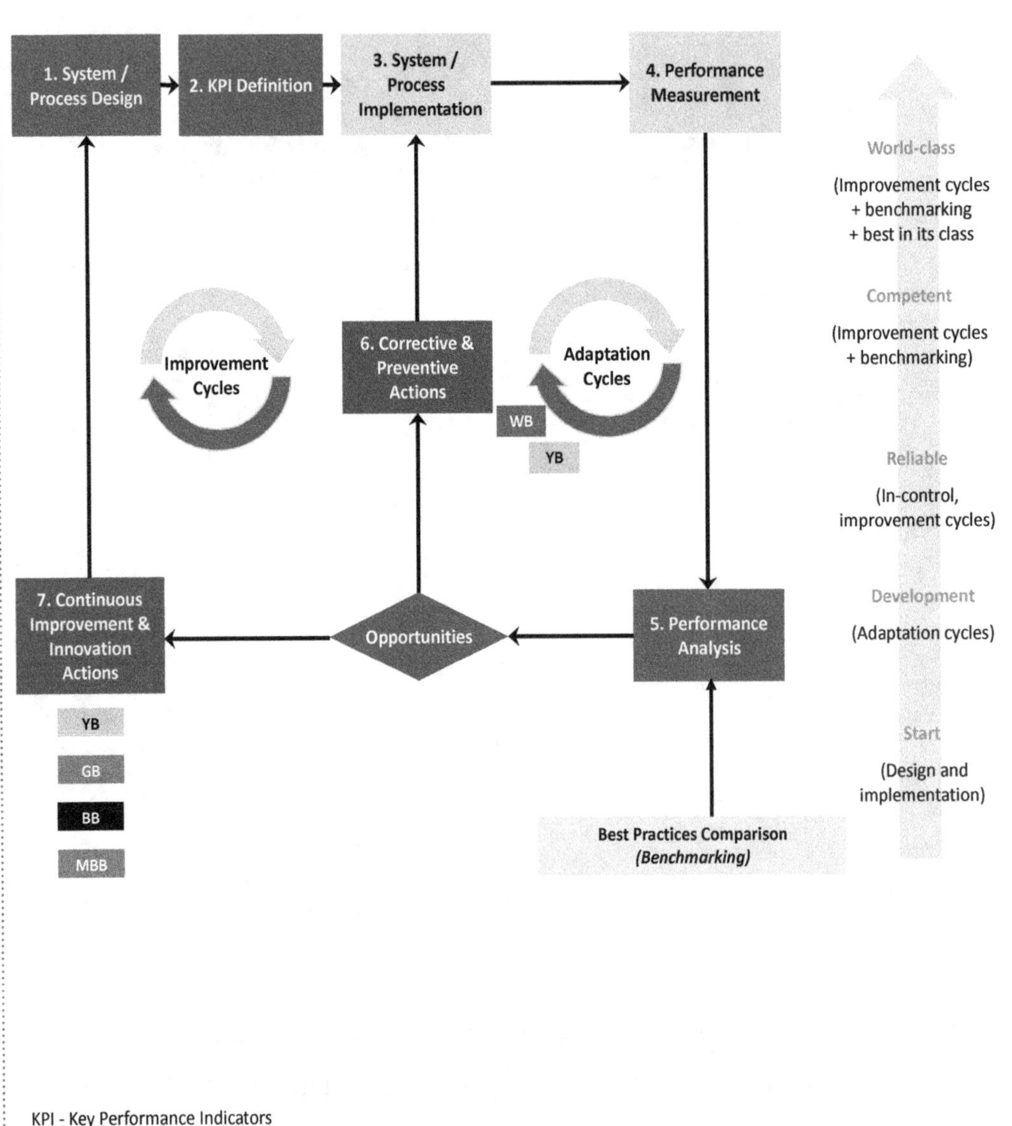

KPI - Key Performance Indicators

LSSI — LEAN SIX SIGMA INSTITUTE

What is Lean & Six Sigma?

Lean = Speed

Improves flow by eliminating waste

Six Sigma = Quality

Improves the process by reducing variation

Lean Six Sigma Model

Goals:
Delight Customers, Sustain Profitability,
Company, Employee, and Societal Benefits

Speed

- Continuous Flow
- TPM
- Theory of Constraints
- Quick Preparations (SMED)
- Pull System

Motivated Team

Focus on the Constraint (TOC)

Quality

- Visual Management *(Andon)*
- Jidhoka
- Error-Proofing *(Poka- Yoke)*
- 6 Sigma
- FMEA
- Problem Solving

Stability: 5S Housekeeping, Visual Management, Standardization, etc.

Leadership: Strategy, Structure, Talent Development, VSM, etc.

LSSI
LEAN SIX SIGMA INSTITUTE

Benefits

Hard Savings

- Reduce Cost
- Increase profit
- Increase demand
- Reduce inventory
- Timely response and delivery
- Increase productivity
- Improve cash flow
- Improve quality
- Reduce defects and rework
- Improve space utilization

Soft Savings

- Improve communication
- Improve customer satisfaction
- Improve customer and employee satisfaction
- Reduce employee turnover
- Improve safety / Reduce risks
- Build a culture of continuous improvement
- Improve decision making

Lean Six Sigma = Breakthrough Results

Lean Six Sigma is applied throughout the company

LEAN SIX SIGMA COMPANY

Upper Management	Human Resources	Research & Development	Sales & Marketing	Accounting & Finance

STRATEGIC TOOLS

Hoshin Kanri
Value Stream Structure
Value Stream Map
Talent Development
Agile Project Management
Standard Work for Leaders
Kata
Gemba Walks

Strategic Tools

All areas use management tools to define, execute and follow up on strategies.

BASIC TOOLS

5S Housekeeping
Visual Management (Andon)
Standardize Work
Personal (Self) Management

Tactical Tools

All areas use basic tools to support identification, development and sustainment of improvements.

LEAN	**SIX SIGMA**

DMAIC

Tool Set

Upper Management	Human Resources	Research & Development	Sales & Marketing	Accounting & Finance
Planning	Talent Attraction	Product Development	Mktg. Campaigns	Budget
				Cost Acct.
Strategic Mgmt.	Talent Development	Lean Startup	Surveys	Inventory
				Payroll
				Invoicing
Decision Making		Design for Six Sigma	Pricing	Credit
				Acct. Payable
			Lean Retail	Financial Statements

LSSI
LEAN SIX SIGMA INSTITUTE

Procurement	Service	Manufacturing	Maintenance	Logistics	Quality	IT

Procurement	Service	Manufacturing	Maintenance	Logistics	Quality	IT
Supplier Development	Lean Service	Lean Manufacturing	Autonomous	Incoming	Quality Deployment	Hardware
				Warehouse		
Purchasing			Preventive	Routing	Quality System	Software
				Loading		
Warehouse			Predictive	Transportation	Calibration	Communication
			Energy			Help Desk

Lean Six Sigma applies to any industry

- Food & Beverage
- Electronics
- Services
- Automotive
- Government
- Agriculture
- Mining
- Packaging
- Airports
- Military

- Pharmaceutical
- Banking
- Insurance
- Hotels
- Restaurants
- Construction

- Healthcare
- Plastics
- Lubricants
- Logistics & Customs
- Education
- Cosmetics
- Footwear
- Textile
- Printing
- Foundry

LEAN MANAGEMENT	WHITE BELT	YELLOW BELT	GREEN BELT	BLACK BELT	MASTER BLACK BELT

Traditional vs. Lean Six Sigma

Traditional

Isolated Projects by departments

Lean Six Sigma

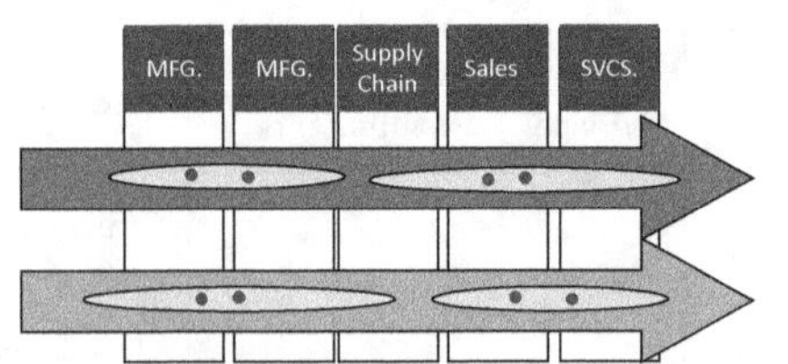

A few high-impact projects in the value stream or service family

*"If I could change the way we implemented it,
I would have started with Lean and then Six Sigma."*

Jack Welch, Ex-CEO GE

LSSI
LEAN SIX SIGMA INSTITUTE

Benefits

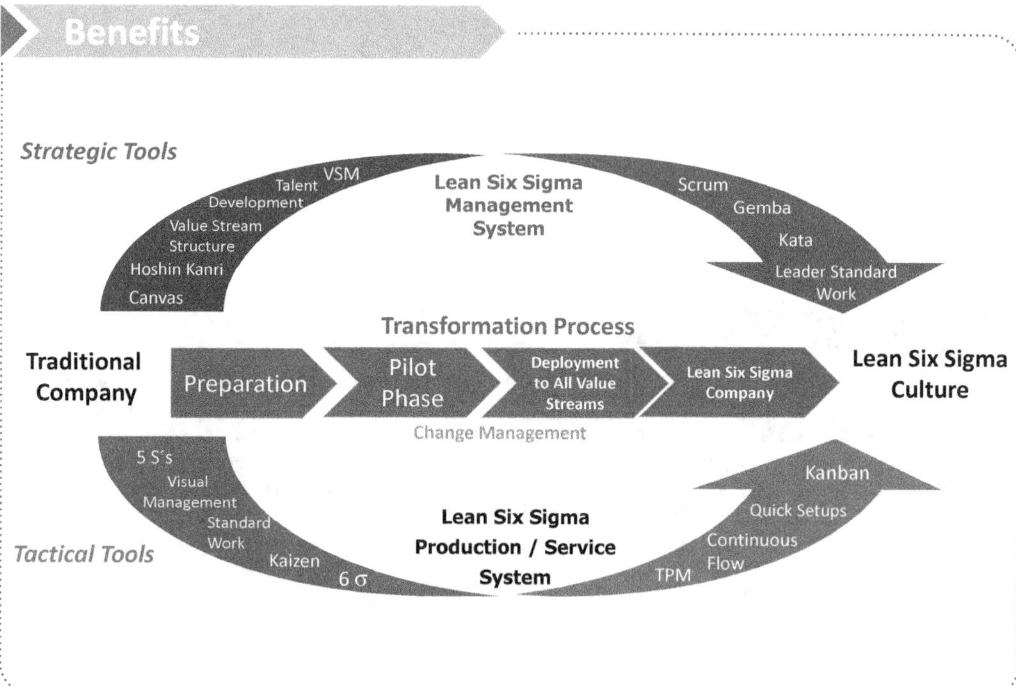

Implementation Process

1 -3 months	4 - 6 months	1 – 2 years	1 – 2 years and onward
Preparation	**Pilot**	**Deployment to All Value Streams**	**Lean Six Sigma Company**

Preparation

- Initial assessment
- Initial training
- Develop Hoshin Kanri
- Define team leader
- Define value stream / service family map
- Select pilot project
- Design initial plan
- Communicate plan
- Kick off

Pilot

Basic Tools
- 5 S Housekeeping, Visual Mgmt., Standard Work, etc.

Improvement and Problem-Solving Tools
- A3, FMEA, Continuous Flow, TPM, SMED, Kanban, Statistics, etc.

Certify
- White and Yellow Belts
- Pilot Process

Deployment to All Value Streams

- Design Value Stream
- Implement VS Office

Deploy to all processes
- Accounting
- Human Resources
- Sales & Marketing
- Logistics
- Service / Production
- IT
- Quality
- Maintenance

Certify
- Yellow, Green & Black Belts
- Value Stream

Lean Six Sigma Company

Certify
- Processes
- Value Streams
- Company / Organization

Change Management - John Kotter

- Analyze the market
- Analyze the competition
- Identify possible risks and opportunities

1. Create a sense of urgency

- Develop the vision
- Develop strategies to carry out the vision

3. Develop a vision & strategy

- Avoid obstacles
- Improve and modify the structure
- Increase risk taking

5. Empower action

- Expand growth to other areas
- Constantly evaluate results
- Support successful processes

7. Consolidate improvements & produce more change

Preparation → **Pilot Phase** → **Deployment to All Value Streams** → **Lean Six Sigma Company**

2. Build a guiding team

4. Communicate the change vision

6. Secure short term gains

8. Make it last

- Form a group of influential and responsible individuals
- Teamwork

- Communicate and share the vision and strategy
- Determine the Team leader

- Plan performance improvements
- Achieve & announce victories
- Reward the responsible parties

- Continue to support the change
- Focus on values and the customer
- Improve management effectiveness

Resistance to change

It has been proven that when facing projects:

20 % +
- 20% of people tend to have a positive attitude towards change.

60 % Neutral
- 60% of people tend to be neutral.

20 % -
- 20% of people tend to have a negative attitude towards change.

If there is good leadership, many who are neutral or negative will become positive. Otherwise, the project may not evolve.

LSSI
LEAN SIX SIGMA INSTITUTE

Why some companies can and others don't?

Vision	+	Skills	+	Incentives	+	Resources	+	Planning	=	Change
X	+	Skills	+	Incentives	+	Resources	+	Planning	=	Confusion
Vision	+	X	+	Incentives	+	Resources	+	Planning	=	Anxiety
Vision	+	Skills	+	X	+	Resources	+	Planning	=	Slow change
Vision	+	Skills	+	Incentives	+	X	+	Planning	=	Frustration
Vision	+	Skills	+	Incentives	+	Resources	+	X	=	False start

Lean Six Sigma certifications

There are four certification categories:

1. People Certification

- Training and certification as:
  - White Belt
  - Yellow Belt
  - Green Belt
  - Black Belt
  - Master Black Belt

2 Projects per year

2. Process Certification

- Evaluate if the processes meet the requirements.
- Make sure that the methods are supported and the tools work.

2 Evaluations per year

3. Value Stream Certification

- All value stream processes have achieved a certain level of progress and people are exercising the correct habits.

2-4 Evaluations per year

4. Company Certification

- The company has a Lean / agile management culture and a leadership team that makes decisions based on facts and data.

2 Evaluations per year

LSSI
LEAN SIX SIGMA INSTITUTE

Certification levels

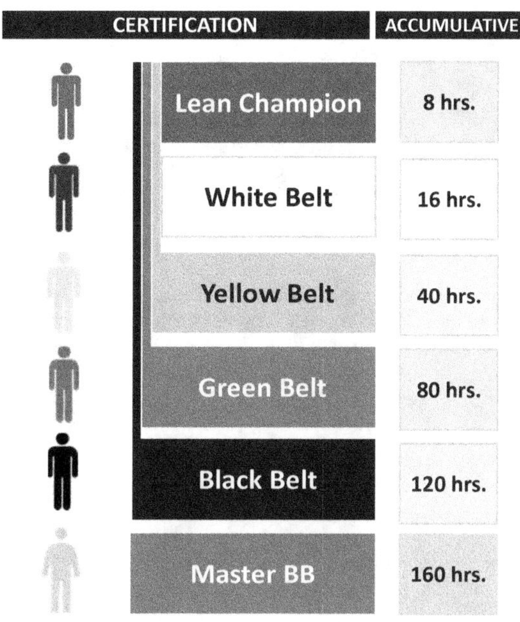

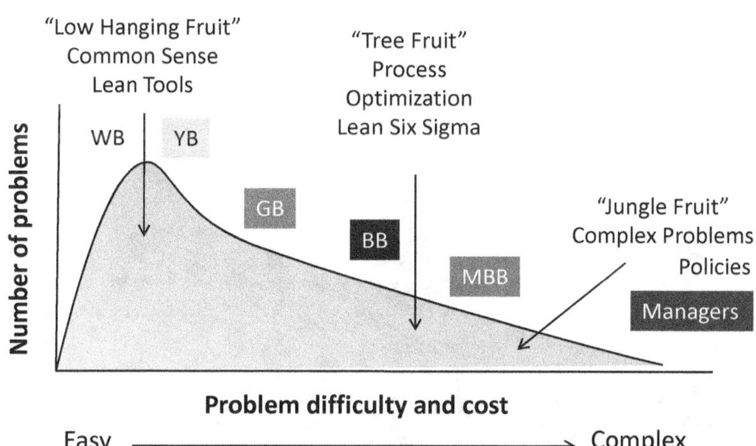

Roles

CHAMPION LSS Management	WHITE BELT	YELLOW BELT	GREEN BELT	BLACK BELT	MASTER BLACK BELT
Responsible for budget and resources	Project Team Member	Lean Practitioner	Small Project Leader who provides specific support	Project Leader & Coach	Experienced Implementation Expert and BB coach
Lean Six Sigma Project Sponsor	Practices the basic tools every day as part of his/her work	Ensures philosophy is sustained on a daily basis	Ensures sustainability in his / her area of responsibility	Ensures correct implementation for the value stream	Expert in practicing Lean Six Sigma throughout the company and supply chain
Leaders	100 %	20 % - 50 %	10 % - 20 %	1 % - 3 %	1 %

Structure

	Executive Staff	Staff	Experts	Selected People
Corporate Office Region Country		 Corporate Champion	Master BB Black Belt	Improvement Teams
Family of Products or Services	Value Stream Teams 	Support Teams  Value Stream Champion	Black Belt Green Belt	Improvement Teams
Productive Teams	Products / Services  	Transactions  Project Champion	Green Belt Yellow Belt	Improvement Teams

LSSI
LEAN SIX SIGMA INSTITUTE

Leadership

Lean Six Sigma requires Leaders

Boss

- Manages employees
- Depends on authority
- Inspires fear
- Says, "I"
- Places blame for breakdowns
- Knows how it is done
- Uses people
- Takes credit
- Commands
- Says, "Go"

Leader

- Coaches employees
- Has goodwill
- Generates enthusiasm
- Says, "We"
- Fixes the breakdowns
- Shows how it is done
- Develops people's talent
- Gives credit
- Asks
- Says, "Let's go"

Conclusion

"No organization, large or small, local or global, is immune to change."

"To address new technological, competitive, and demographic forces, leaders from all sectors are trying to fundamentally alter the way their organizations do business."

John P. Kotter

Canvas

Learning objectives

1. Understand the importance of business models in developing new ideas and in contributing new ways to develop business strategy.
2. Understand the elements that form part of it.
3. Identify opportunities for implementation.
4. Understand how it is developed.

Content

> Background
> What is Canvas?
> Who uses Canvas?
> Elements
> Examples
> Procedure
> Exercise

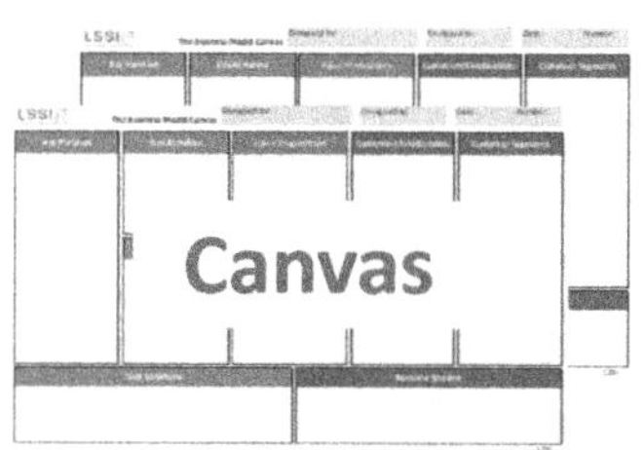

Successful execution

Make it simple!!

TOP MANAGEMENT				MANAGEMENT PLANNING			
Objectives	Indicators	Baseline	Objective	Strategies	Indicators	Baseline	Objective
1. Increase profitability	Increase ROI from 7 to 12%	7%	12%	1.1 Increase profit/revenue to 18% 1.2 Increase RONA to 24%	Inventory Value Conversion costs Materials cost	24 M 1950 990 K	16 M 1500 K 900 K
Increase sales	Increase domestic sales by 15% and international sales by 32%	10% 29%	15% 32%	2.1 Sell services that add value to our customers 2.2 Increase sales with current customers 2.3 Launch new products in record time 2.4 Enter new niche markets	NPS Revenue Days to launch new products Market Share	55% 4.5 M 123 12%	70% 5 M 45 15%
3. Become a world-class company (reduce expenses)	Increase profitability of the operation from 25% to 45%, reducing defects and improving customer satisfaction, cost reduction of 11%	25% Cost 2	45% > 11% 0	 Strategy 3.2 Maintain ISO 9000:2000 certification 3.3 Implement New Information System	Facility sigma level Ontime deliveries OEE Delivery days Inventory Value Inventory turns Conversion Costs Cost of poor quality Number of nonconformities On time implementation	3.3 78% 53% 12 24 M 4 2.1 M 125 K 3	4.2 99% 78% 8 16 M 12 1.25 M 12 K 0 9
4. Make HR a competitive advantage	Achieve less than 1% annual turnover	7%	1%	3.1 Establish a suggestions program	Certification progress Suggestions per person Safety - Days without accidents	21% -	78% 1

Value Stream Structure

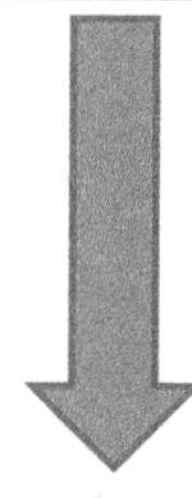

BOX SCORE	Objective	1 13-may	2 20-may
Units per person	21	14,00	16,00
On-time deliveries	100%	100%	100%
Lead time (days)	4	3	4
Days from door to door	3	6	12
First pass quality	95%	80%	80%
Sigma level	5	4,10	4,30
Quality costs	$ 250	$ 2.345	$ 3.112
Average product cost		$ 343	$ 337
Inventory value		$ 3.004.234	$ 2.334.756
Inventory turns		4,50	4,00
Maintenance costs		$ 2.820	$ 645
5S Evaluation	100%	100%	100%
OEE	85%	70%	73%
Demand		500	600,00
Production Capacity		650	650,00
Available capacity		23%	8%
Revenue		$ 432.050	$ 384.870
Material Costs		$ 189.000	$ 125.679
Conversion Costs		$ 131.200	$ 130.242
Value Stream Profit		$ 111.850	$ 128.949
Value Stream ROS		25,89%	33,50%

Results

Key activities/Improvement projects	1	2	3	4	5	6	7	8	9	4
1.1 Reduce inventory to 2 M										
1.2 Find investments options										
1.3 Find new vendors to reduce material cost										
1.4 Implement Lean Cost Accounting										
2.1.1 Design customer service packages										
2.1.2 Analyze purchase frequency a										
2.3.1 Develop product a for market X										
2.3.1 Implement lean design										
3.1.1 Train personnel on Six Sigma										
3.1.2 YB, GB, BB certification										
3.1.3 Executive training										
3.1.2 Pilot implementation in area A										
3.1.2 Certify personnel as multiskille										
3.1.3 Implement Lean Accounting										
3.1.4 Implement Lean Logistics pilot										
3.1.5 Implement Lean Product Development										
3.1.6 Implement Lean Quality system										

Project Portfolio

Origin

Alex Osterwalder

The Business Model Ontology – A Proposition in a Design Science Approach

January 2004

PhD Thesis, University of Lausanne, Switzerland

LSSI
LEAN SIX SIGMA INSTITUTE

Is Canvas for you?

- Do you have an entrepreneurial spirit?
- Are you constantly thinking about how to create value and develop new business?
- Are you constantly thinking about how to improve or transform your organization?
- Are you looking for innovative ways to do business to replace old or obsolete ones?

Not everyone has a clear understanding of what a business model is.

Strategic conversations about business models are unproductive.

Typical conversation when there is no common language:

- Director: The world is changing ... we urgently need to reinvent our business model.
- Person 1: We should focus on services.
- Person 2: The numbers indicate that we should grow in emerging markets.
- Person 3: But, what about the new technology that we have been looking for?
- Director: In fact, I know the right person to acquire that technology.

3 hours later.....

- Person 2: bla bla bla bla.
- Person 4: bla bla bla bla.
- Person 1: bla bla bla bla.
- Person 3: bla bla bla bla.

What is Canvas?

It is a visual and practical business tool to **describe**, **test**, **implement**, and **manage** business models during their life cycle.

Who uses Canvas?

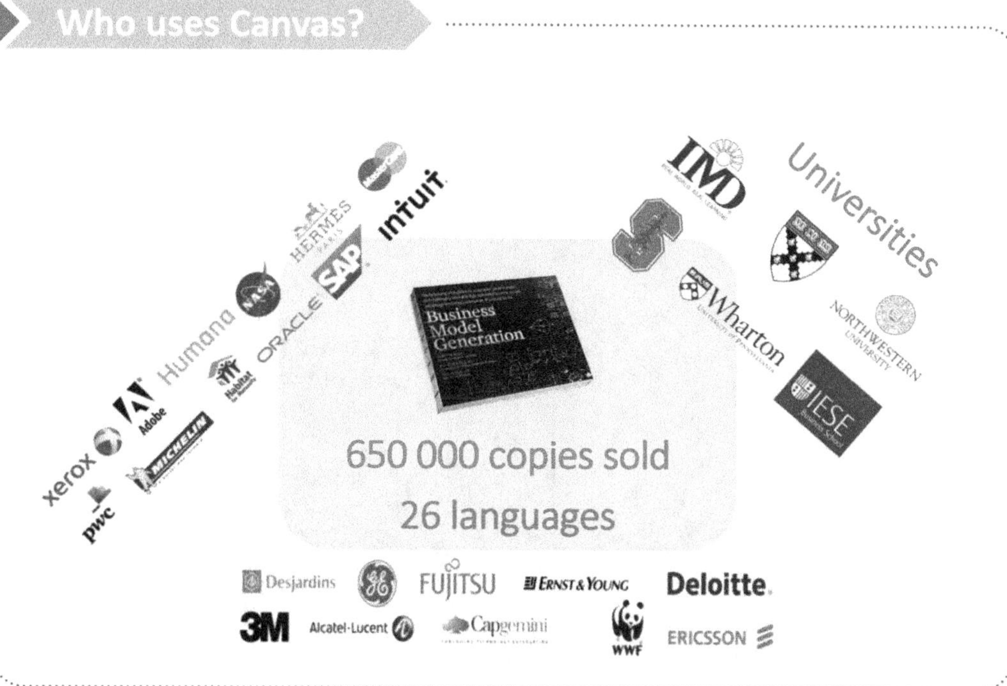

What types of professionals use Business Model Canvas?

- **Directors, Executives and Managers:** Manage business and organizations

- **Entrepreneurs:** Develop new business and organizations

- **Employees:** Sustain and improve business models

- **Consultants:** Help their clients

- **Designers:** Create high value products

- **Investors:** Evaluate business opportunities

Your business model on one page

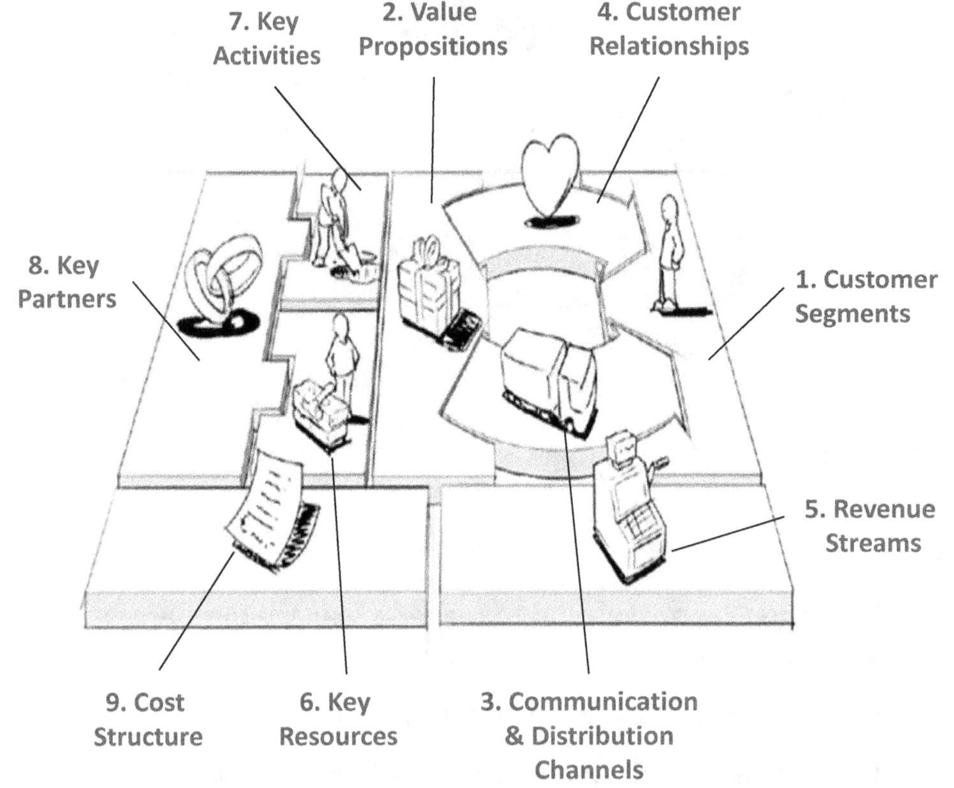

LSSI
LEAN SIX SIGMA INSTITUTE

Business Model Canvas Template

LSSI
LEAN SIX SIGMA INSTITUTE

The Business Model Canvas

| Designed for: | Designed by: | Date: | Number: |

Key Partners

Suppliers and partners that make the model of business work

Key Activities

What activities and processes should be carried out to produce the value proposition?

Key Resources

What are the key assets to make the business model work?

Value Propositions

What value do we deliver to the customer?
Which one of our customer's problems are we helping to solve?
What bundles of products and services are we offering to each customer segment?
Which customer needs are we satisfying?

Customers Relationships

What kind of relationships do we establish so that the customer stays tied to the value offer even after having acquired it?

Channels

How will we make the client receive our value proposition?

How to deliver the product or service?

Customer Segments

For whom do we create value?

Cost Structure

What costs are significant to operate the business model?

Revenue Streams

What kind of profits will the business have?

Canvas is designed like the human brain

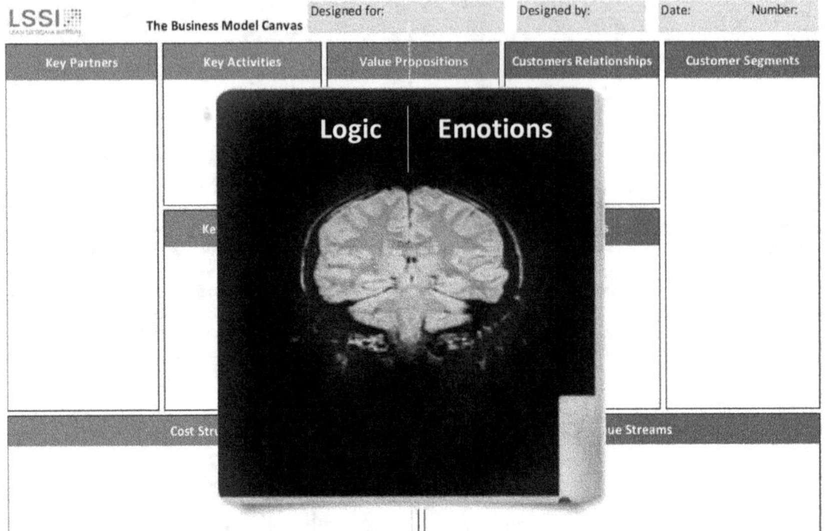

Another way to see it

Backstage

Frontstage

LSSI
LEAN SIX SIGMA INSTITUTE

Why use Canvas?

- The best ideas are put on the table

- Create a common and shared language

- Improve teamwork with better conversations about strategies

- Promotes collaboration between areas

- Creates a structured and practical approach that helps to implement ideas for improvement

Examples

Google was founded in 1998

Revenue 2017 = $109.65 Billions US Dollars

- Larry Page and Sergey Brin
- They created the Google search engine
- It is free!
- So, how to make money from a free service?

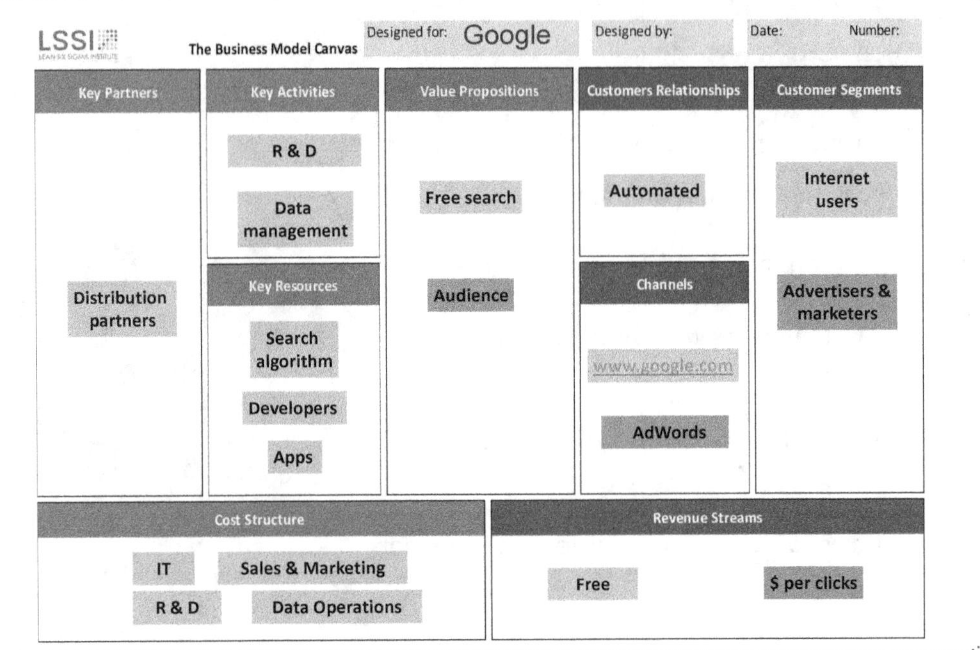

Xerox 1958

- They invented a machine that could photocopy 2000 copies a day when the competition could do 30 to 40 copies a day.

- The machine was 7 times more expensive.

- They did a market study and they found that no customer would buy such an expensive machine.

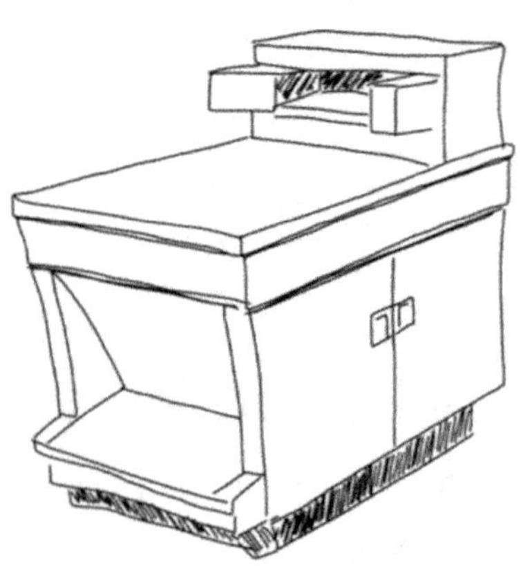

Great product! Wrong business model

LSSI
LEAN SIX SIGMA INSTITUTE

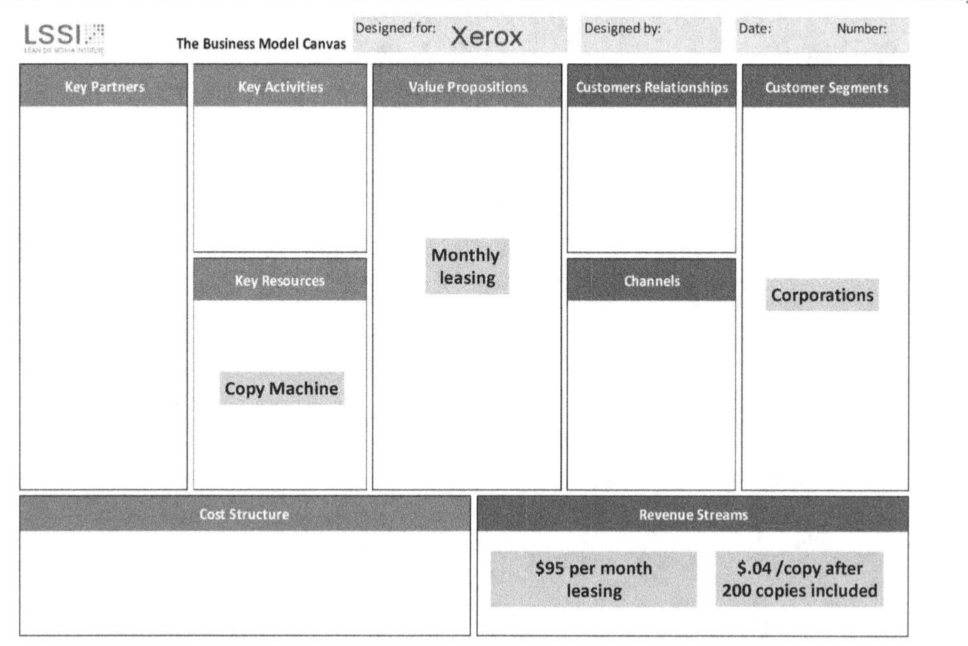

Procedure

How is it develop?

- Choose a business product / service

- Teams of 5 people

- **Structure of the Canvas:**

1. Introduction to the methodology
2. Current Canvas
3. Research environment around the current canvas:
   - Market trends
   - Technology trends
   - Needs Trends
   - Strengths and weaknesses
4. Generate future canvas prototypes
5. Feedback
6. Define future Canvas and next steps

Implementation phases

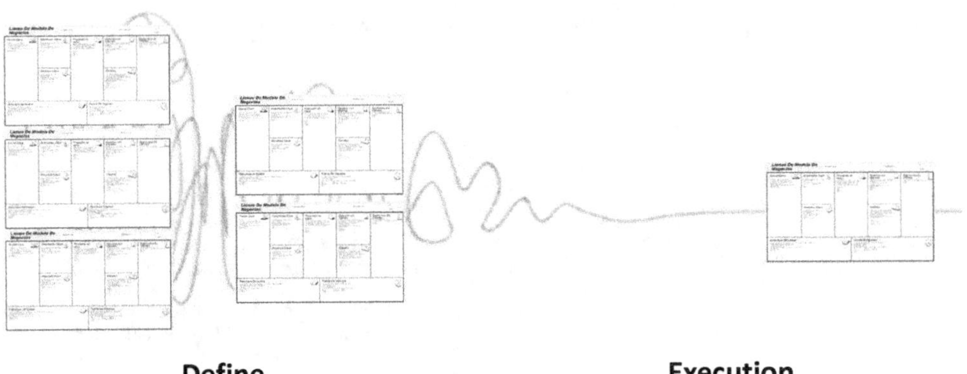

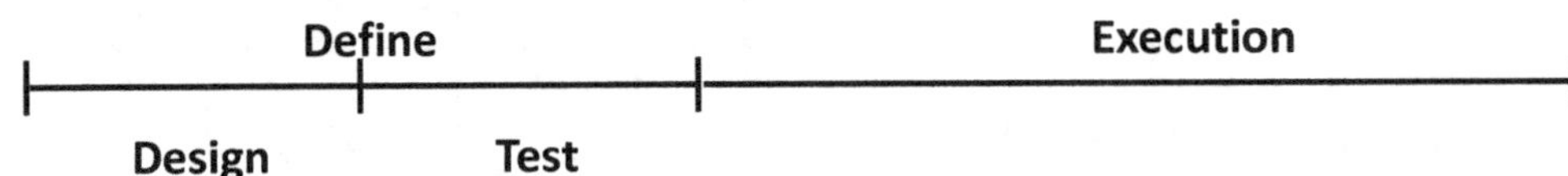

Design	**Test**

Define   **Execution**

Note

- Several business models can be generated for each line of business.

- To make it effective, only those that can be executed must be chosen. Generally, great enthusiasm is generated in the creation of the model.

- Make sure you keep that enthusiasm in the execution.

LSSI
LEAN SIX SIGMA INSTITUTE

- Develop the Nespresso business model with the elements shown on the next slide.

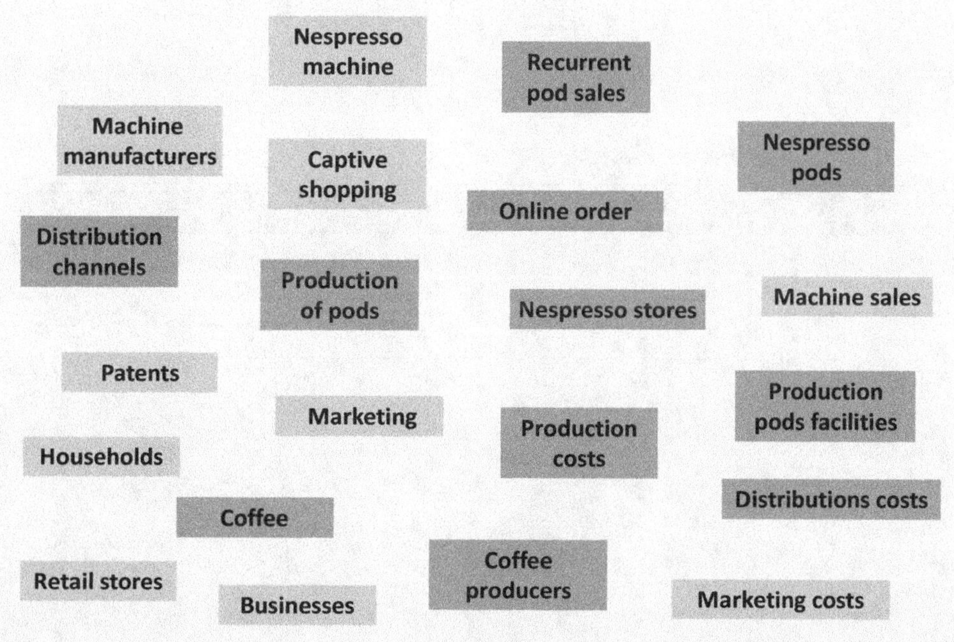

LSSI
LEAN SIX SIGMA INSTITUTE

The Business Model Canvas

Designed for: **Nespresso**   Designed by: Date: Number:

Key Partners	Key Activities	Value Propositions	Customers Relationships	Customer Segments
	Key Resources		**Channels**	

Cost Structure	Revenue Streams

LSSI
LEAN SIX SIGMA INSTITUTE

Lean Strategy:
Hoshin Kanri

Learning objectives

1. Understand the key elements of Strategic Planning.
2. Understand the Hoshin Kanri implementation process.
3. Start the Hoshin Kanri planning process in a company.

Content

> Background
> What is Hoshin Kanri?
> Benefits
> When is it used and how long does it take?
> Procedure
> Example

Background

- Only between 10% and 20% of companies in the world create a strategic plan.

- Only between 10% and 20% execute the plan successfully.

- 91% of executives qualify as "exceptional decision-makers".

Source: Harvard Business School.

Symptoms of companies in need of Hoshin Kanri planning

- No connection between strategy and continuous improvement

- Too many projects in process

- The plans from one year to the next never seem to connect

What is strategy?

Strategy

Strato = A group of people
E.g. Army

Agein = Guide
E.g. Direct

"Art of conducting military operations."

LSSI
LEAN SIX SIGMA INSTITUTE

Strategy deployment

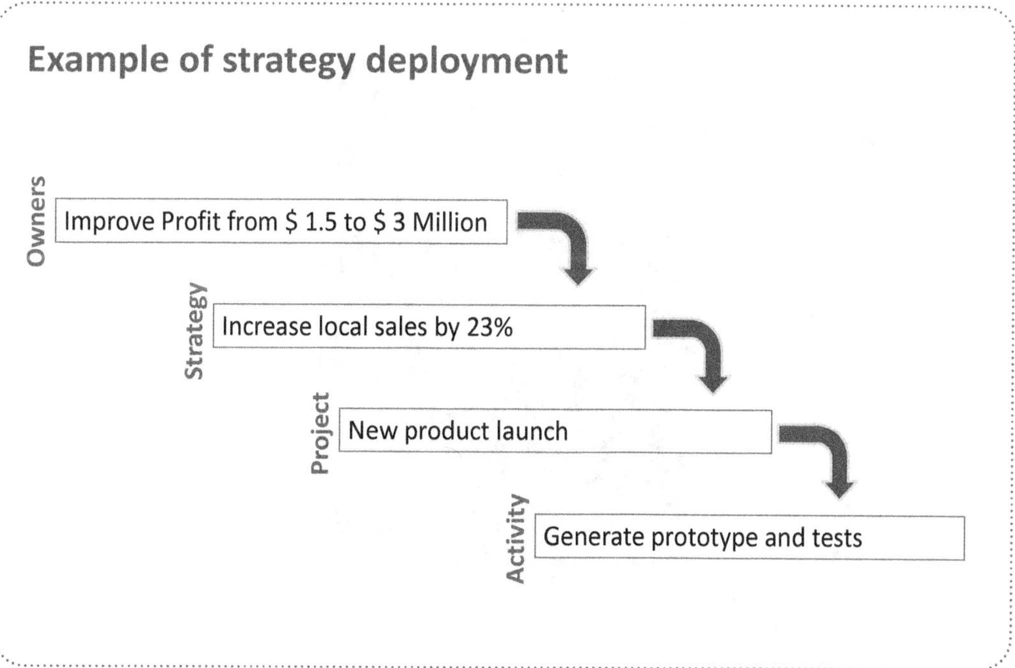

DFSS (Design for Six Sigma)

Example of strategy deployment

What is Hoshin Kanri?

Hoshin is a management tool to address 4 fundamental questions:

- **What is it about?** - vision and key results areas.

- **How will we measure our performance?** - key metrics and objectives.

- **What are we going to do?** - strategies, action plans.

- **How will we behave?** - core values.

LSSI
LEAN SIX SIGMA INSTITUTE

Meaning of hoshin kanri

Hoshin kanri

ho = Direction

kan = Control

shin = Needle

ri = Reason or logic

hoshin = Direction of needle or compass

kanri = Administration control

方針

管理

Hoshin kanri means management and control
of an organization's direction or focus.

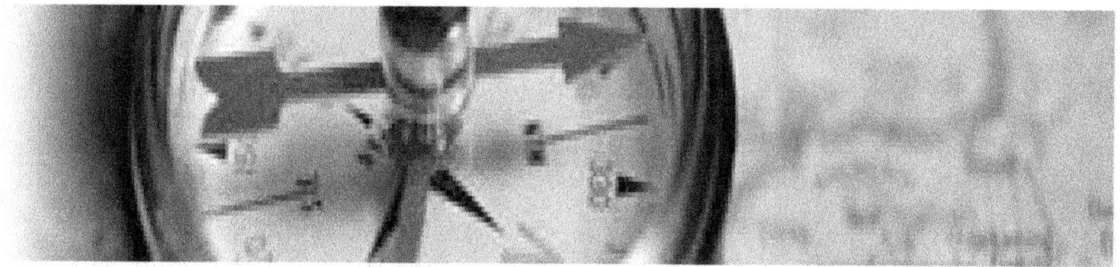

Hoshin Kanri model

Year: 2019-2022	Company Name:

Philosophy

Vision: Achieve the best market value by offering the best quality at the lowest

Mission: To develop, produce, and distribute high-quality products and services.

Values: Customer Commitment, Quality, Respect for people, Integrity, Teamwork.

Date Prepared:

GUIDELINES		MANAGEMENT PLANNING		
Objectives	Indicators	Strategies	Indicators	Person Responsible
1. Guidelines (What's)	4. Indicators (How much)	2. Strategies (How's)	4. Indicators (How much)	

LSSI
LEAN SIX SIGMA INSTITUTE

Strategic Plan: HOSHIN KANRI

Date Revised:

	PROJECTS														
Key activities/Improvement projects		1	2	3	4	5	6	7	8	9	10	11	12	Progress	Leader

3.
Projects
(How's of strategies)

5.
Resources
(Who)

Other terms used for Hoshin Kanri

- Hoshin Planning (Hewlett-Packard)

- Policy Deployment (AT&T, Infineon Technologies)

- Policy Management (Texas Instruments)

- Management by Results (Xerox)

- Priority Management

- Goals Deployment

- "Catch-ball" Process

- **Focuses** the whole company on a few **vital goals**, instead of the many trivial ones.

- Creates **alignment** towards objectives through the **participation** of the entire management team in the planning process.

- **Leadership** at **all** levels.

- **Communicates** key goals to all managers and staff.

- **Integrates and encourages** inter-functional cooperation to achieve significant progress. A review process that holds participants accountable for achieving their part of the plan.

When is it used and how much time does it require?

- **Start of operations:** fundamental plan (Hoshin Kanri and Box score).
  - Realization time: **1 week**
- **Annually:** update of the fundamental plan (Hoshin Kanri).
  - Realization time: **2-4 days**
- **Monthly:** evaluation of global progress (balanced scorecard).
  - Realization time: **1 hour**
- **Weekly:** evaluation of value streams (box score).
  - Realization time: **30 minutes**
- **Daily:** evaluation of progress per hour (process board).
  - Realization time: **5 minutes**

Procedure

LSSI
LEAN SIX SIGMA INSTITUTE

1. Establish the philosophy of the company

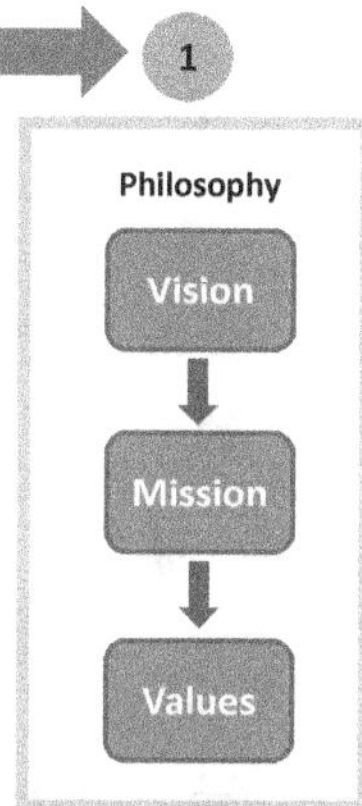

VISION
What do we want to be?

MISSION
What is our business?
Why do we exist?

VALUES
**What do we believe in and
how do we behave?**

Examples of vision / mission

Disney's mission: "We create happiness by providing the finest entertainment for people of all ages, anywhere."

Google's mission: "Organize world information so that it is universally accessible and useful."

eBay's mission: "Providing a global electronic market in which virtually anyone can trade with almost any product, thus creating economic opportunities throughout the world."

Apple's vision: "We believe that we are on the face of the earth to make great products and that's not changing ."

Nike's vision: "Bring inspiration and innovation to every athlete in the world. If you have a body, you are an athlete."

Example of philosophy

1 Philosophy

HOSHIN KANRI

Year
2019-2022

Philosophy

Vision: Achieve the best market value by offering the best quality at the lowest cost

Mission: To develop, produce and distribute reliable and delicious food products

Values: Customer Commitment, Quality, Respect for people, Integrity, Teamwork

TOP MANGEMENT		MANAGEMENT PLANNING
Objectives (Whats)	Indicators (How many whats)	Strategies (Hows) - Whats

LSSI
LEAN SIX SIGMA INSTITUTE

Strategic Plan

Slogan

Date Prepared

Date Revised

Indicators (How many hows)	Person Responsible

EXECUTION

Key activities/Improvement projects	Leader

2. Establish objectives (what's)

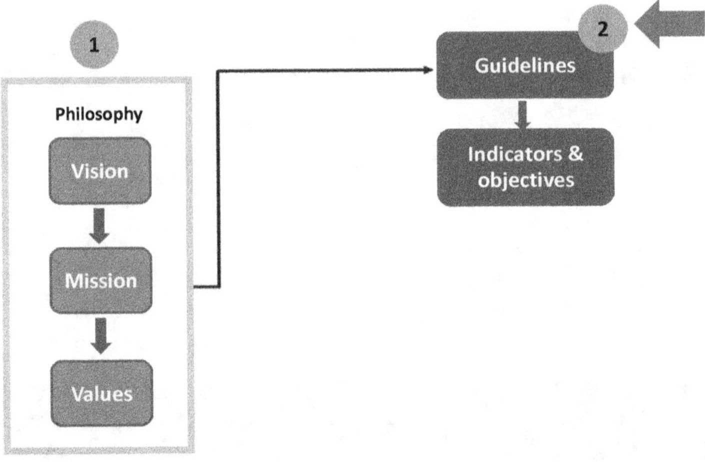

- In this phase, the organization's essential and functional categories must be identified in order to improve their performance.

- It provides a basis for identifying critical issues that must be analyzed before establishing short-term objectives – which eventually build into a long-term vision and objectives.

- We must answer the following questions:

    - **What value proposition(s) do customers expect from us?**

    - **What results does management expect from us?**

    - **What must we accomplish in order to build towards the future state we aim to become?**

LSSI
LEAN SIX SIGMA INSTITUTE

Establish objectives (what's)

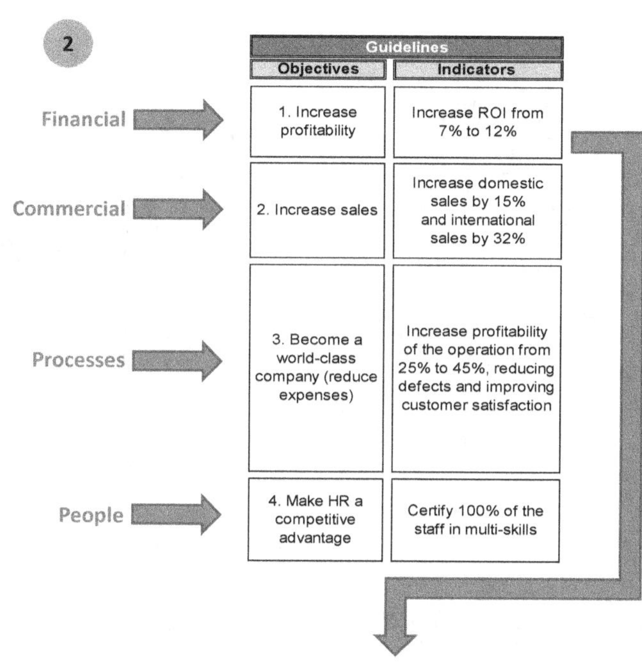

Example: DuPont Model

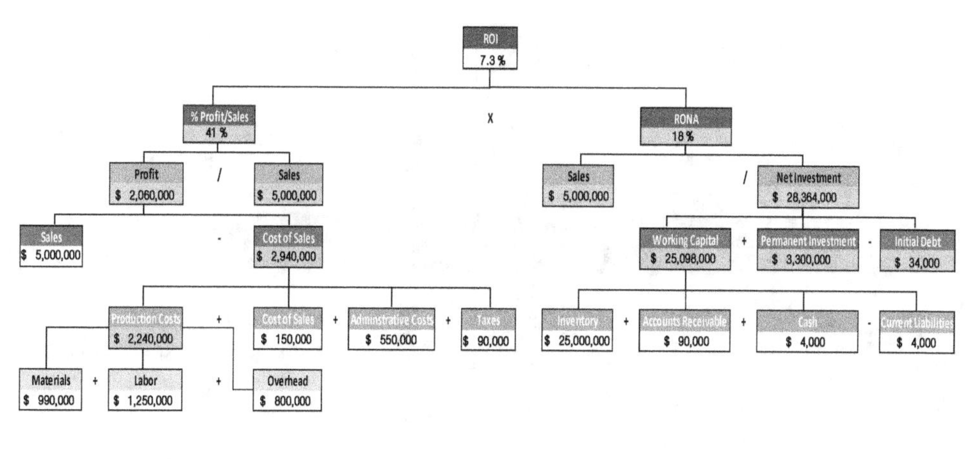

Indicators and objectives of the guidelines

Balanced Scorecard

Monthly Executive Indicator

Guidelines	Objectives	Goal	(YTD)	January	February	Ma...
Financial	Economic Value Added	4%				
	ROI	12%				
	RONA	18%				
	$ Backlog	$100,000				
	Throughput	$4,010,000				
	Cash Flow	$800,000				
Commercial	Profit / Loss	$2,060,000				
	Revenue	$5,000,000				
	Net Promoter Score	78%				
	Market Share	22%				
Processes	Conversion Costs	$1,250,000				
	Direct Cost	$990,000				
	Inventory Value	$650,000				
	Total Investment	$27,364,000				
People	Internal NPS	90%				
	Employee engagement	90%				
	Turnover	1%				
	Talent Development	85%				

3. Development of strategies

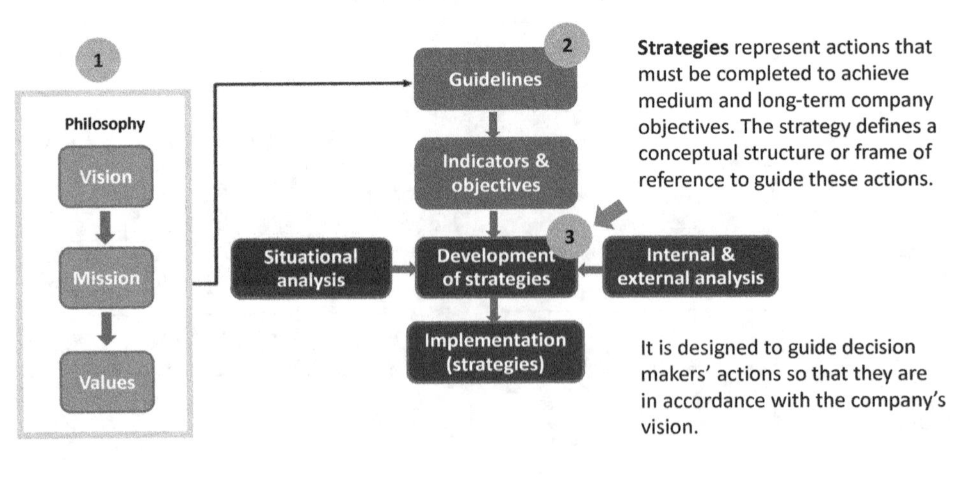

Strategies represent actions that must be completed to achieve medium and long-term company objectives. The strategy defines a conceptual structure or frame of reference to guide these actions.

It is designed to guide decision makers' actions so that they are in accordance with the company's vision.

Example of development of strategies

GUIDELINES		MANAGEMENT PLANNING		
Objectives	Indicators	Strategies	Indicators	Person Responsible
1. Increase profitability	Increase ROI from 7% to 12%	1.1 Increase profit / sales to 18% 1.2 Increase sales to 24%	Profits / sales Sales / investments	VT, MK, DG VT, MK, DG VT, MK, IN
2. Increase sales	Increase domestic sales by 15% and international sales by 32%	2.1 Sell services that add value to our customers 2.2 Increase sales with current customers 2.3 Launch products in record time 2.4 Enter new niche markets	Sales in $ NPS Days to launch Targeted segments	VT, MK, DG VT, MK, DG VT, MK, IN
3. Become a world-class company (reduce expenses)	Increase profitability of the operation from 25% to 45%, reducing defects and improving customer satisfaction	3.1 Implement Lean Company	Facility sigma level Level of customer satisfaction OEE Delivery days Inventory turns Operation expenses % scrap	IN, CA, DG, RH IN, CA, DG, RH IN, CA, DG, RH IN, CA, DG, RH IN, CA, DG, RH IN, CA, DG, RH IN, CA, DG, RH
		3.2 Maintain ISO 9000:2000 certification	Number of nonconformities	CA All
		3.3 Implement lean logistics	On-time deliveries (punctuality)	CA, SE, DG All IN, CAL
4. Make HR a competitive advantage	Certify 100% of the staff in multi-skills	4.1 Establish talent development program	% progress of the program % of certified personnel	HR

3

Strategies "HOW'S"

SWOT Matrix

Method: **SWOT Matrix**	Strengths 1. 2. 3.	Weaknesses 1. 2. 3.
Opportunities 1. 2. 3.	Use the strengths to take advantage of the opportunities	Overcome weaknesses while taking advantage of opportunities
Threats 1. 2. 3.	Use the strengths to avoid threats	Minimize weaknesses and avoid threats

4. Indicators

Balanced Scorecard: monthly Indicator

BALANCED SCORECARD

Guidelines	Objectives	Goal	(YTD)	January	February	March	April	May
Financial	Economic Value Added	4%						
	ROI	12%						
	RONA	18%						
	$ Backlog	$100,000						
	Throughput	$4,010,000						
	Cash Flow	$800,000						
Commercial	Profit / Loss	$2,060,000						
	Revenue	$5,000,000						
	Net Promoter Score	78%						
	Market Share	22%						
Processes	Conversion Costs	$1,250,000						
	Direct Cost	$990,000						
	Inventory Value	$650,000						
	Total Investment	$27,364,000						
People	Internal NPS	90%						
	Employee engagement	90%						
	Turnover	1%						
	Talent Development	85%						

Tracking the Value in the floor:
Day-by-the-hour board

Goal 73 units
Capacity 10 units per hour
Date: 01/01/20

Hours	Goal	Actual	Accumulated	Downtime (minutes)	Type	Defects
8 to 9	10	10	10			
9 to 10	8	7	17	10	Break	
10 to 11	10	10	27			
11 to 12	10	5	32	20	Setups	
12 to 1	5	4	36	30	Lunch	
1 to 2	10	11	47			
2 to 3	10	2	49	30	Breakdown	3
3 to 4	10	11	60			
Total	73	60		90		3

LSSI — LEAN SIX SIGMA INSTITUTE

- The **indicators** help us understand the real functioning of the system, as they serve as a translator of what happens in the operation and tell us if the strategies and / or projects lead to an established objective.

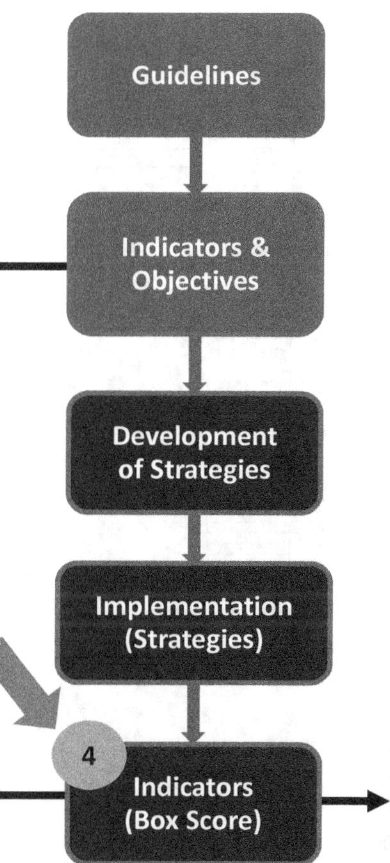

Box Score: weekly Indicator

BOX SCORE	Objective	13-May	20-May	27-May	3-Jun	10-Jun	17-Jun
Units per person	21	14.00	16.00	18.00	20.00	19.00	23.00
On-time deliveries	100%	100%	100%	100%	100%	100%	100%
Lead time (days)	4	3	4	1	3	4	5
Days from door to door	3	6	12	23	14	9	7
First pass quality	95%	80%	80%	80%	85%	85%	85%
Sigma level	5	4.10	4.30	4.11	4.32	4.70	4.34
Quality costs	$ 250	$ 1,125	$ 2,320	$ 645	$ 345	$ 1,245	$ 3,124
Average product cost	$ 300	$ 343	$ 337	$ 362	$ 338	$ 337	$ 325
Inventory value	$ 545,000	$ 3,004,234	$ 2,334,756	$ 2,945,893	$ 2,564,392	$ 1,945,678	$ 1,234,975
Inventory turns	12	4.50	4.00	6.70	7.10	8.30	9.00
Maintenance costs	$ 500	$ 2,820	$ 645	$ 2,323	$ 976	$ 1,733	$ 756
5S Evaluation	100%	100%	100%	100%	100%	100%	100%
OEE	85%	70%	73%	75%	79%	81%	81%
Demand		500	600.00	550.00	495.00	620.00	545.00
Production Capacity		650	650.00	650.00	650.00	650.00	650.00
Available capacity		23%	8%	15%	24%	5%	16%
Revenue		$ 432,050	$ 384,870	$ 422,456	$ 389,754	$ 389,455	$ 456,032
Material Costs		$ 189,000	$ 125,679	$ 167,453	$ 133,456	$ 133,234	$ 197,034
Conversion Costs		$ 131,200	$ 130,242	$ 132,000	$ 132,426	$ 128,034	$ 111,342
Value Stream Profit		$ 111,850	$ 128,949	$ 123,003	$ 123,872	$ 128,187	$ 147,656
Value Stream ROS		25.89%	33.50%	29.12%	31.78%	32.91%	32.38%

Integration of indicators

Organization

BALANCED SCORECARD

Guidelines	Objectives	Goal	(YTD)
Financial	Economic Value Added	4%	
	ROI	12%	
	RONA	18%	
	$ Backlog	$100,000	
	Throughput	$4,010,000	
	Cash Flow	$800,000	
Commercial	Profit / Loss	$2,060,000	
	Revenue	$5,000,000	
	Net Promoter Score	78%	
	Market Share	22%	
Processes	Conversion Costs	$1,250,000	
	Direct Cost	$990,000	
	Inventory Value	$650,000	
	Total Investment	$27,364,000	
People	Internal NPS	90%	
	Employee engagement	90%	
	Turnover	1%	
	Talent Development	85%	

Value Stream 1

	Base Line	Goal	Weeks 1	2	3	4	5	6	7	8	9	10
NPS	55%	70%										
Revenue	4.5 M	5 M										
Days to launch new products	123	45										
Market Share	12%	15%										
Facility sigma level	3.3	4.2										
Ontime deliveries	78%	99%										
OEE	53%	78%										
Delivery time (days)	12	8										
Inventory Value	24 M	16 M										
Inventory turns	4	12										
Conversion Costs	2.1 M	1.25 M										
Cost of poor quality	125 K	12 K										
Sigma Level												
Number of nonconformities	3	0										
On time implementation												
Certification progress	21%	78%										
Sugestions per person	-	1										
Accidents	3	0										
Demand	2500 K	3000 K										
Production Capacity	3000 K	3500 K										
Available capacity												
Inventory Value	24 M	16 M										
Revenue	4.5	5 M										
Material Costs	990 K											
Conversion Costs	1950 K	00 K										
Value Stream Profit												
Value Stream ROS												

Cell 1

Total Goal	78		Date	2/7/15

Capacity: 10 per hour

Hour	Goal	Real	Down Time min.	Type	Defects
8 to 9	10	10			
9 to 10	8	7	10	Break	
10 to 11	10	10			
11 to 12	10	5	20	Setup	
12 to 1	5	4	30	Lunch	
1 to 2	10	11			
2 to 3	10	2	30	Breakdown	3
3 to 4	10	11			
	73	60	90		3

Cell 2

Total Goal	78		Date	2/7/15

Capacity: 10 per hour

Hour	Goal	Real	Down Time min.	Type	Defects
8 to 9	10	10			
9 to 10	8	7	10	Break	
10 to 11	10	10			
11 to 12	10	5	20	Setup	
12 to 1	5	4	30	Lunch	
1 to 2	10	11			
2 to 3	10	2	30	Breakdown	3
3 to 4	10	11			
	73	60	90		3

LSSI — LEAN SIX SIGMA INSTITUTE

January	February	March	April	May

Value Stream 2

	Base Line	Goal	1	2	3	4	5	6	7	8	9	10
NPS	55%	70%										
Revenue	4.5 M	5 M										
Days to launch new products	123	45										
Market Share	12%	15%										
Facility sigma level	3.3	4.2										
Ontime deliveries	78%	99%										
OEE	53%	78%										
Delivery time (days)	12	8										
Inventory Value	24 M	16 M										
Inventory turns	4	12										
Conversion Costs	2.1 M	1.25 M										
Cost of poor quality	125 K	12 K										
Sigma Level												
Number of nonconformities	3	0										
On time implementation												
Certification progress	21%	78%										
Sugestions per person	-	1										
Accidents	3	0										

	Base Line	Goal										
Demand	2500 K	3000 K										
Production Capacity	3000 K	3500 K										
Available capacity												

	Base Line	Goal										
Inventory Value	24 M	16 M										
Revenue	4.5	5M										
Material Costs		900 K										
Conversion Costs	1950 K	1500 K										
Value Stream Profit												
Value Stream ROS												

Cell 1

Cell 2

Cell 1

Total Goal	78		Date	2/7/15
Capacity	10	per hour		

Hour	Goal	Real	Down Time min.	Type	Defects
8 to 9	10	10			
9 to 10	8	7	10	Break	
10 to 11	10	10			
11 to 12	10	5	20	Setup	
12 to 1	5	4	30	Lunch	
1 to 2	10	11			
2 to 3	10	2	30	Breakdown	3
3 to 4	10	11			
	73	60	90		3

Cell 2

Total Goal	78		Date	2/7/15
Capacity	10	per hour		

Hour	Goal	Real	Down Time min.	Type	Defects
8 to 9	10	10			
9 to 10	8	7	10	Break	
10 to 11	10	10			
11 to 12	10	5	20	Setup	
12 to 1	5	4	30	Lunch	
1 to 2	10	11			
2 to 3	10	2	30	Breakdown	3
3 to 4	10	11			
	73	60	90		3

Box Score – weekly indicators

BOX SCORE	Objective	1 13-May	2 20-May
Units per person	21	14.00	16.00
On-time deliveries	100%	100%	100%
Lead time (days)	4	3	4
Days from door to door	3	6	12
First pass quality	95%	80%	80%
Sigma level	5	4.10	4.30
Quality costs	$ 250	$ 1,125	$ 2,320
Average product cost	$ 300	$ 343	$ 337
Inventory value	$ 545,000	$ 3,004,234	$ 2,334,756
Inventory turns	12	4.50	4.00
Maintenance costs	$ 500	$ 2,820	$ 645
5S Evaluation	100%	100%	100%
OEE	85%	70%	73%
Demand		500	600.00
Production Capacity		650	650.00
Available capacity		23%	8%
Revenue		$ 432,050	$ 384,870
Material Costs		$ 189,000	$ 125,679
Conversion Costs		$ 131,200	$ 130,242
Value Stream Profit		$ 111,850	$ 128,949
Value Stream ROS		25.89%	33.50%

- The results of quality, delivery, and costs are analyzed weekly to ensure that they are studied and decisions can be made weekly.

- Now there are **52 opportunities** to make good decisions, contrary to only 12 when it is done monthly.

LSSI
LEAN SIX SIGMA INSTITUTE

3		4		5		6	
27-May		3-Jun		10-Jun		17-Jun	
18.00		20.00		19.00		23.00	
100%		100%		100%		100%	
1		3		4		5	
23		14		9		7	
80%		85%		85%		85%	
4.11		4.32		4.70		4.34	
$	645	$	345	$	1,245	$	3,124
$	362	$	338	$	337	$	325
$ 2,945,893		$ 2,564,392		$ 1,945,678		$ 1,234,975	
6.70		7.10		8.30		9.00	
$	2,323	$	976	$	1,733	$	756
100%		100%		100%		100%	
75%		79%		81%		81%	

550.00	495.00	620.00	545.00
650.00	650.00	650.00	650.00
15%	24%	5%	16%

	3		4		5		6
$	422,456	$	389,754	$	389,455	$	456,032
$	167,453	$	133,456	$	133,234	$	197,034
$	132,000	$	132,426	$	128,034	$	111,342
$	123,003	$	123,872	$	128,187	$	147,656
29.12%		31.78%		32.91%		32.38%	

Color codes

Prompt attention

Good

Alert

5. Development of tactics

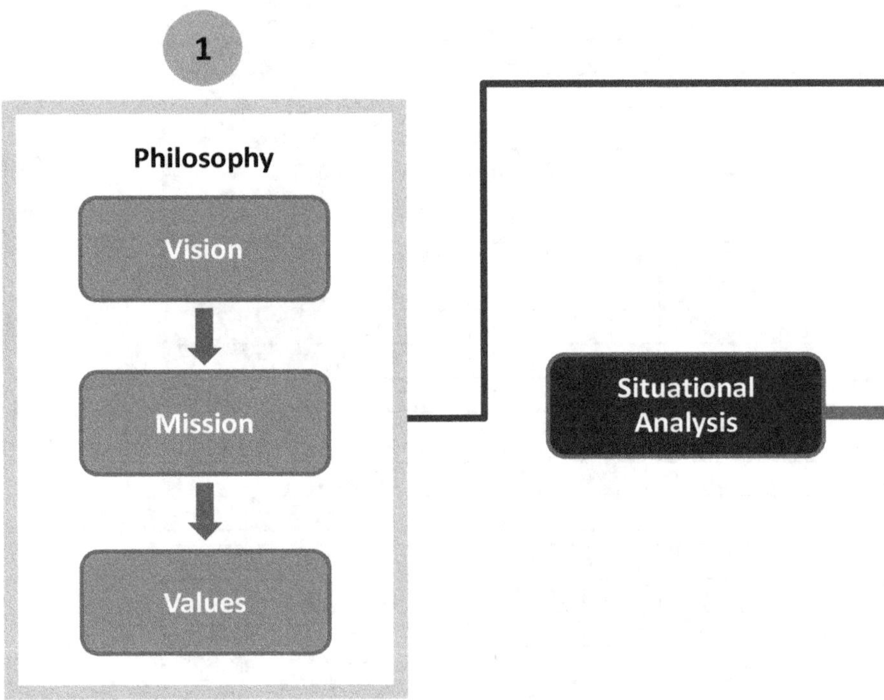

Tactical planning refers to the key projects and activities that must be carried out to comply with established strategies.

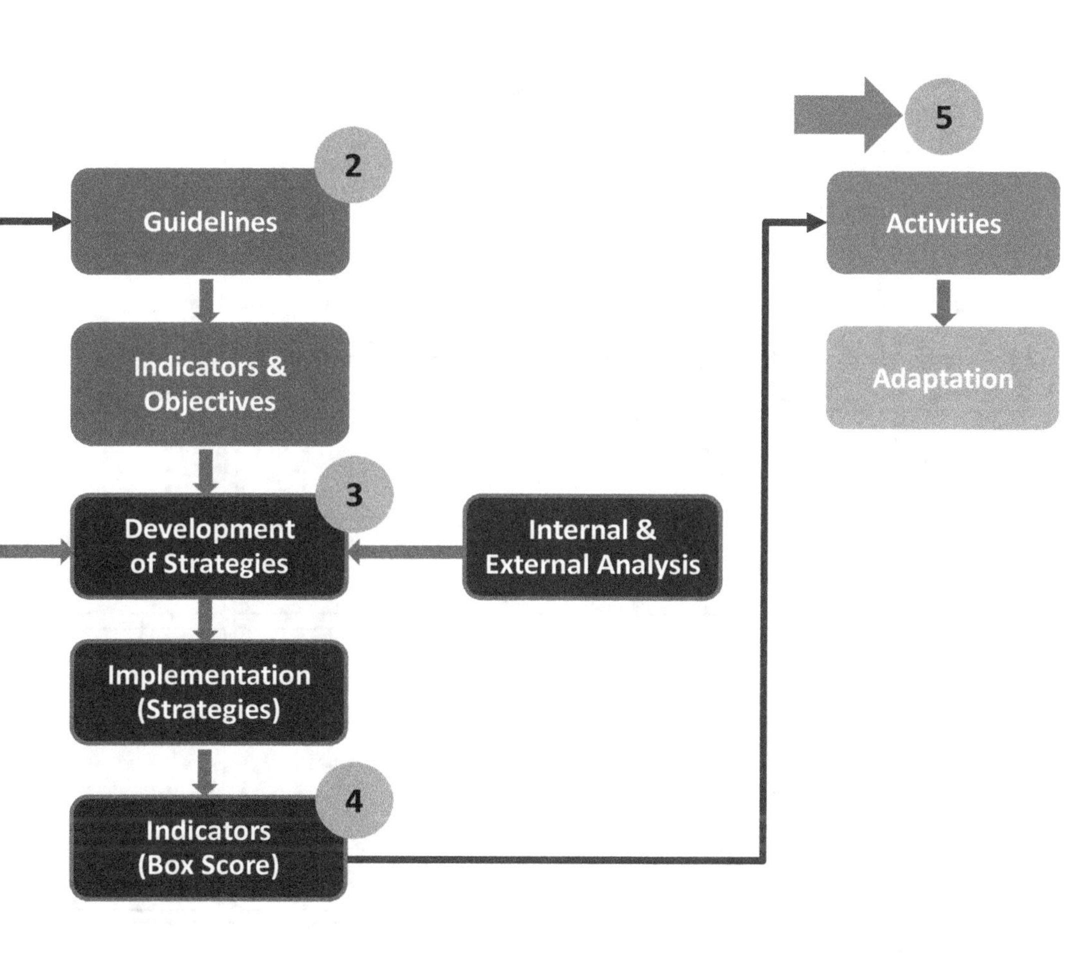
2
Guidelines
Indicators &
Objectives
3
Development
of Strategies
Internal &
External Analysis
Implementation
(Strategies)
4
Indicators
(Box Score)
5
Activities
Adaptation

Example of development of tactics

Year
2019-2022

HOSHIN KANRI

Philosophy

Vision: Achieve the best market value by offering the best quality at the lowest cost

Mission: To develop, produce and distribute reliable and delicious food products

Values: Customer Commitment, Quality, Respect for people, Integrity, Teamwork

GUIDELINES		MANAGEMENT PLANNING		
Objectives	Indicators	Strategies	Indicators	Person Responsible
1. Increase profitability	Increase ROI from 7% to 12%	1.1 Increase profit / sales to 18% 1.2 Increase sales to 24%	Profits / sales Sales / investments	VT, MK, DG VT, MK, DG VT, MK, IN
2. Increase sales	Increase domestic sales by 15% and international sales by 32%	2.1 Sell services that add value to our customers 2.2 Increase sales with current customers 2.3 Launch products in record time 2.4 Enter new niche markets	Sales in $ NPS Days to launch Targeted segments	VT, MK, DG VT, MK, DG VT, MK, IN
3. Become a world-class company (reduce expenses)	Increase profitability of the operation from 25% to 45%, reducing defects and improving customer satisfaction	3.1 Implement Lean Company	Facility sigma level Level of customer satisfaction OEE Delivery days Inventory turns Operation expenses % scrap	IN, CA, DG, RH IN, CA, DG, RH IN, CA, DG, RH IN, CA, DG, RH IN, CA, DG, RH IN, CA, DG, RH IN, CA, DG, RH
		3.2 Maintain ISO 9000:2000 certification	Number of nonconformities	CA All
		3.3 Implement lean logistics	On-time deliveries (punctuality)	CA, SE, DG All IN, CAL
4. Make HR a competitive advantage	Certify 100% of the staff in multi-skills	4.1 Establish talent development program	% progress of the program % of certified personnel	HR

LSSI
LEAN SIX SIGMA INSTITUTE

LSSI
LEAN SIX SIGMA INSTITUTE

Slogan

Date Prepared

Date Revised

Key activities/Improvement projects	PROJECTS												Progress	Leader
	1	2	3	4	5	6	7	8	9	10	11	12		
1.1 Reduce inventories														
1.2 Improve the use of our investments														
1.3 Reduce costs without sacrificing quality														
1.4 Achieve an agile costing to detect variations														
2.1 Design customer service packages														
2.2 Analyze purchase frequency and identify trends														
2.3 Implement SCRUM for product development														
2.4 Introduce concurrent engineering and DFSS														
3.1.1 Train personnel on Six Sigma														
3.1.2 YB, GB, BB certification														
3.1.3 Executive training														
3.1.4 Pilot implementation in area A														
3.1.5 Certify personnel as multiskilled operators														
3.1.6 Implement 5S in facility 1														
3.1.7 Implement TPM in the pilot area														
3.1.8 Implement continuous flow in the pilot														
3.1.9 Implement SMED in the pilot area														
3.2.1 Conduct internal audits														
3.2.2 Perform all corrective actions														
3.3.1 Implement kanban														
3.3.2 Implement heijunka														
3.3.3 Implement software														
4.1.1 Conduct a diagnosis of the organizational climate														
4.1.2 Train Coaches														
4.1.3 Develop training materials														
4.1.4 Perform pilot implementation														

5

Tactics

Example of development of tactics

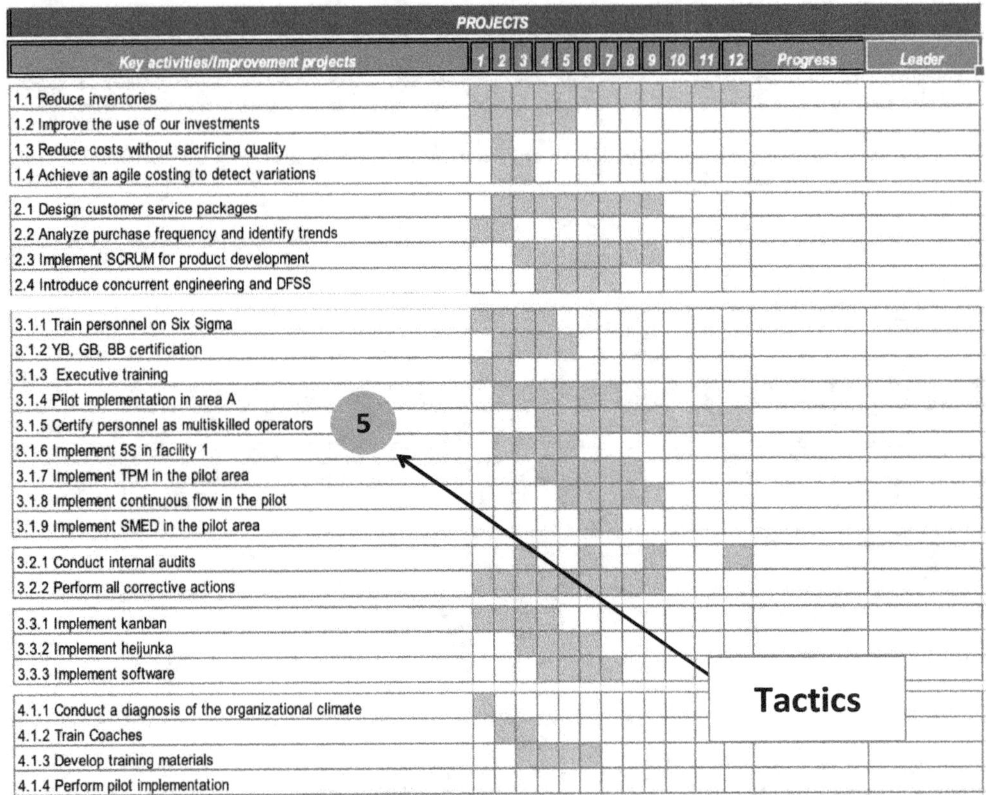

- Once the tactical planning has been defined, work on the development of the projects can begin.

- To ensure that the strategy is executed, these projects must be successfully carried out through an agile management system called **SCRUM.**

Note: Scrum is a tool that will be reviewed during the Black Belt certification

Value Stream Structure

Teamwork is possible if the structure is right

Learning objectives

1. Understand how companies of the future will be designed by value streams.
2. Show how self-managed teams can perform.
3. Understand the basic concepts of Lean Accounting in value streams.

Content

> Background
> What is value stream structure?
> Why implement value streams?
> Who participates?
> Procedure
> Example

Background

A company that has decided to be agile in response to the client's needs, and is sufficiently productive to stay in the market, should consider:

- Direct and effective communication

- A flat and agile organization

- Teamwork

A good strategic plan is not enough

Strategic Plan

Hoshin Kanri

Structure

Value Stream

Follow up

Results (box score)
Projects

Traditional organization structure

- Companies are traditionally organized by departments and use structures similar to family trees.

- Currently many companies are still organized in this way.

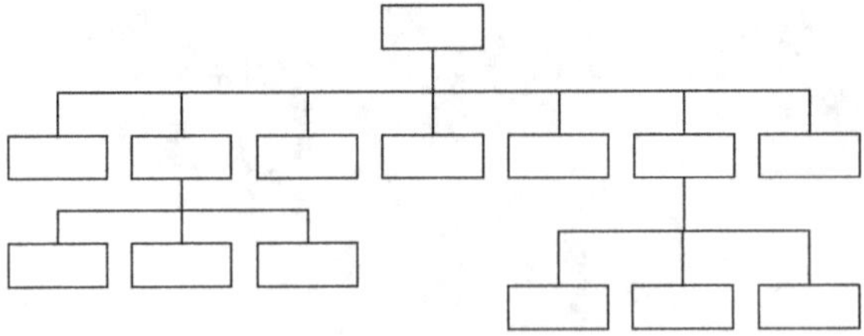

- These systems work relatively well in high-volume, low-mix product or service environments.

LSSI
LEAN SIX SIGMA INSTITUTE

Example of traditional structure

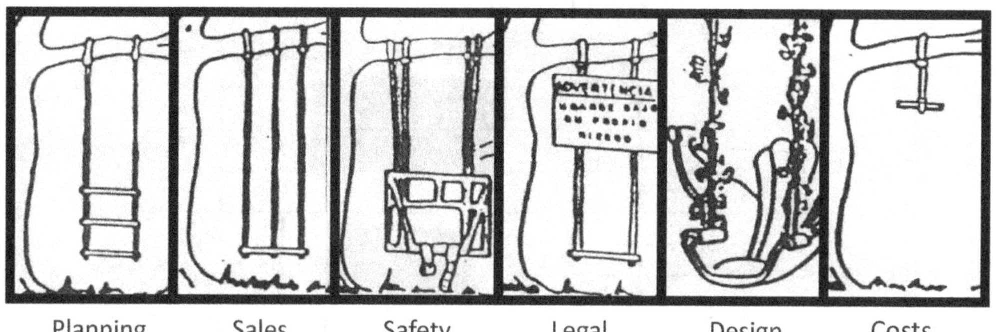

Planning   Sales   Safety   Legal   Design   Costs

Engineering   Manufacturing   Packaging   Marketing   Service   Client needs

Organizational structure types

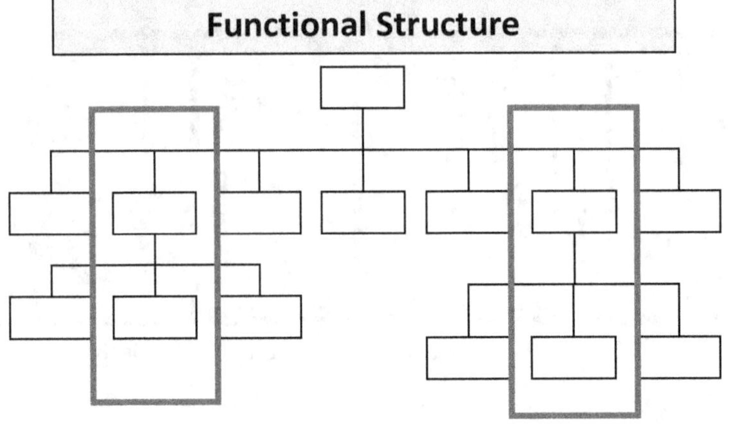

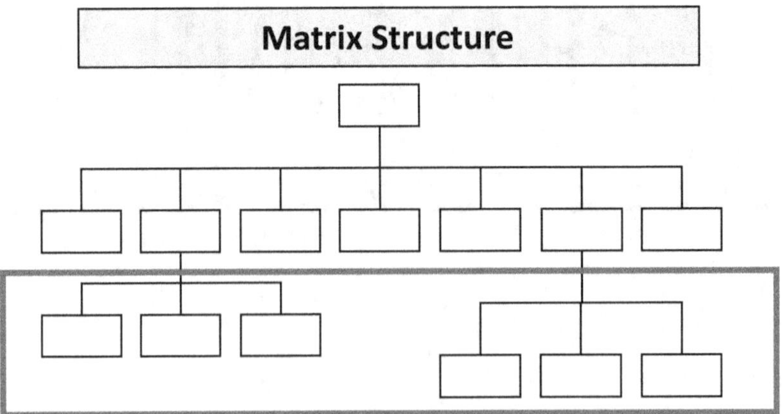

LSSI
LEAN SIX SIGMA INSTITUTE

Departmental Structure

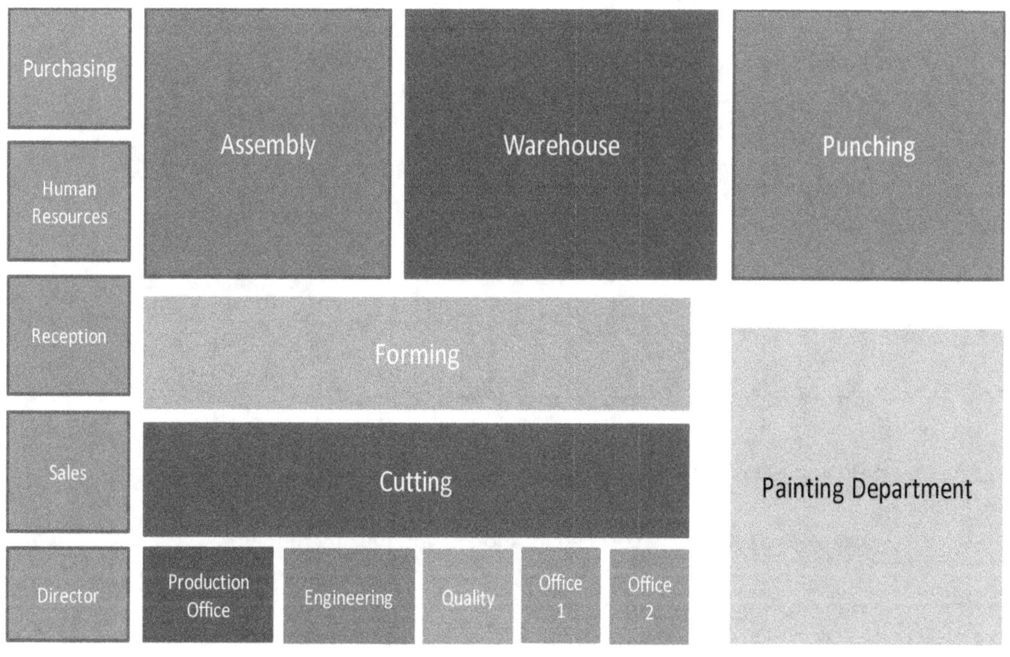

Conclusions

▸ Managers delegated poorly or tried to solve problems at all levels.

▸ Lower-level staff simply received orders and didn't always understand why they were doing certain activities.

▸ It was rare that everyone involved in the processes could answer the following questions:

- At what speed the customer is willing to buy? (Takt-time)

- What is the companies' capacity?

- Where is the main constraint?

- Are we delivering our products or services on time?

- Do you really know what the customer thinks about your products?

- Are you reaching the costs goals and are you making money?

- Does everybody knows the same?

LSSI — LEAN SIX SIGMA INSTITUTE

What is value stream structure?

A value stream structure is a business unit that:

* Is composed of all those directly responsible for the activities of a family of products or services.

* Is comprised of cross functional teams that continually analyze available information and execute any necessary changes.

Each value stream will be analyzed through a map (VSM), where you will see the process flow of information, activities and materials.

"The way companies of the future are being designed."

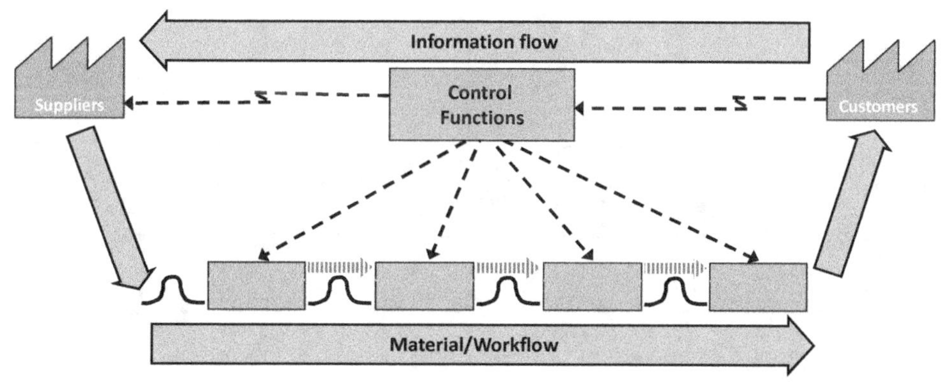

Value stream structure

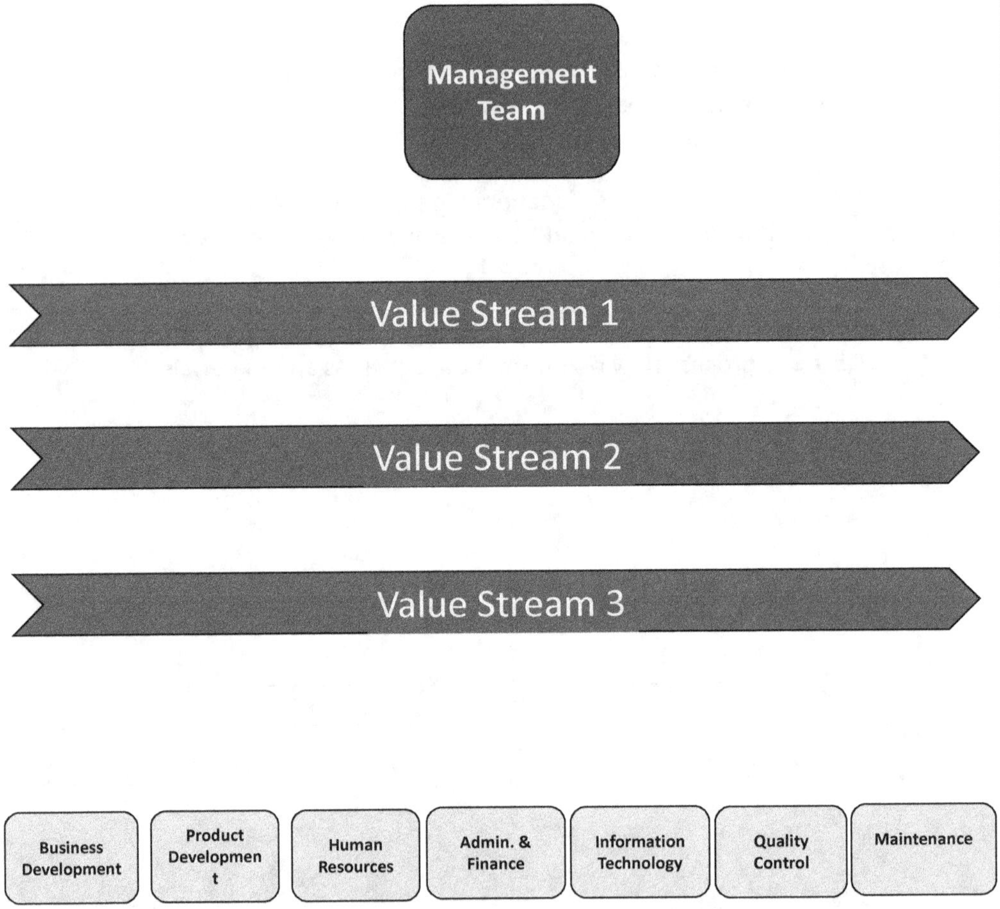

Management Team

Value Stream 1

Value Stream 2

Value Stream 3

| Business Development | Product Development | Human Resources | Admin. & Finance | Information Technology | Quality Control | Maintenance |

Each value stream represents a product or service family.

LSSI
LEAN SIX SIGMA INSTITUTE

Why implement value streams?

- To eliminate all the bureaucracy that prevents to develop successful businesses.

- It gives management time to plan, analyze the future of the business, and devote more energy to future development.

- It allows strategies such as Lean Six Sigma to be successful.

Who participates?

Level 3: Owners and Directors

Level 2: Value Stream Teams and Support

Level 1: Production or Service Teams

Procedure

1. Define **level 1** staff and train them on their roles (standardized work).

2. Define **level 2** staff and train them on their roles (leader standard work).

3. Design the value office and boards for the reviews of each level (Andon, Leader Standard Work, etc.)

4. Analyze the performance of the value stream:

   A. Update the box score and floorboards

   B. Value stream cost analysis

5. Design how the **level 3** (management team) will work, if the pilot was successful in the deployment phase.

LSSI
LEAN SIX SIGMA INSTITUTE

1. Define level 1 staff and train them on their roles

Level 1 responsibilities

▸ **Leaders, operators, material handlers, and technicians**

- Conduct meetings at the beginning and end of a shift

- Daily planning and hourly analysis of progress

- Team-based decision making

- Analyze their own results

- Solve problems

Update the day by-the-hour board

Goal	73 units
Capacity	10 units per hour

Date: 01/01/20

Hours	Goal	Actual	Accumulated	Downtime (minutes)	Type	Defects
8 to 9	10	10	10			
9 to 10	8	7	17	10	Break	
10 to 11	10	10	27			
11 to 12	10	5	32	20	Setups	
12 to 1	5	4	36	30	Lunch	
1 to 2	10	11	47			
2 to 3	10	2	49	30	Breakdown	3
3 to 4	10	11	60			
Total	**73**	**60**		**90**		**3**

LSSI
LEAN SIX SIGMA INSTITUTE

2. Define level 2 staff and train them on their roles

Level 2 responsibilities

› **Value stream manager, financial analyst, customer service representative, sales associate, scheduler, manufacturing engineer, quality analyst, etc.**

- Work in the "value office"
- Weekly planning and review of box score
- Daily analysis of obligations, profitability, potential problems and requirements
- Daily analysis of results
- Take action
- Solve level 2 problems
- Support level 1

› **Support areas: HR, Maintenance, IT, etc.**

- They work in their processes as internal service providers
- Weekly planning
- Daily analysis of box score results, responsibilities, profitability, and potential problems
- Take action
- Solve level 2 problems

Value stream board

Value stream board: name

Strategy

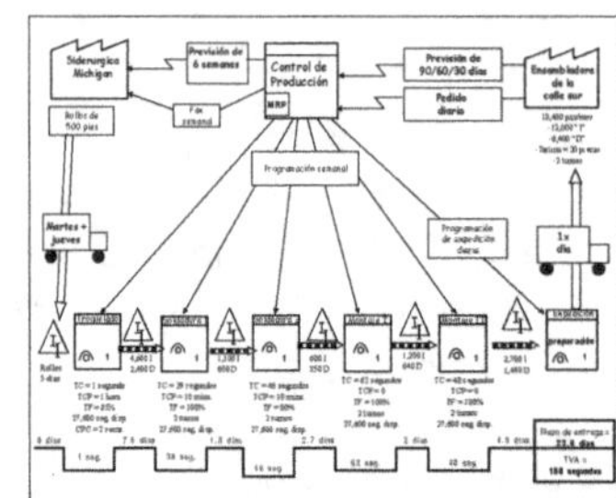

Current VSM

Structure

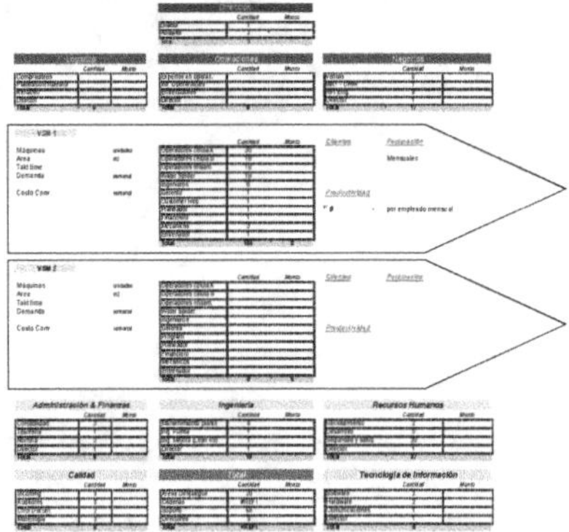

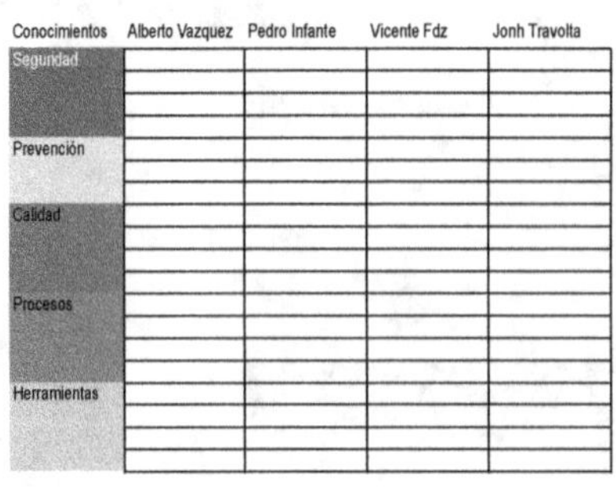

Muda Analysis

1. Unbalanced production
2. $1,000,000 excess inventory
3. Transports- 2 km
4. Movement 14 km
5. Defects 9%
6. Overburden: 560 hours of OT
7. Variability: Cpk = 1.1
8. OEE= 49%
9. Changeover times > 4 hours

Talent Development

Conocimientos	Alberto Vazquez	Pedro Infante	Vicente Fdz	Jonh Travolta
Seguridad				
Prevención				
Calidad				
Procesos				
Herramientas				

Opportunity cards

LSSI
LEAN SIX SIGMA INSTITUTE

Future VSM

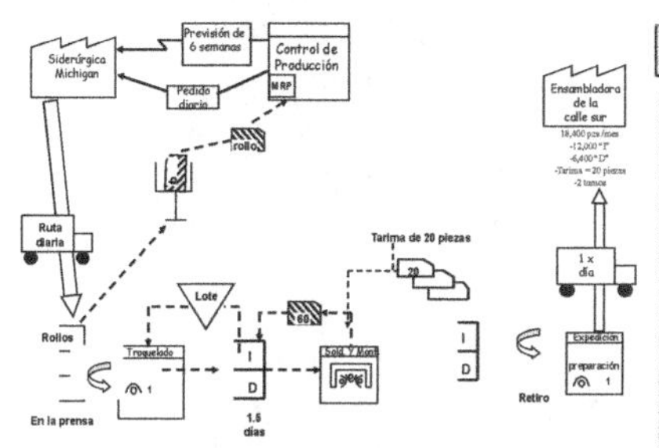

Kaizen program

1. TPM Event   April 5th
2. SMED Event   May 22nd
3. Cell manufacturing event June 1st
4. Energy Savings event   July 2nd
5. Sigma kaizen July 16th

Results

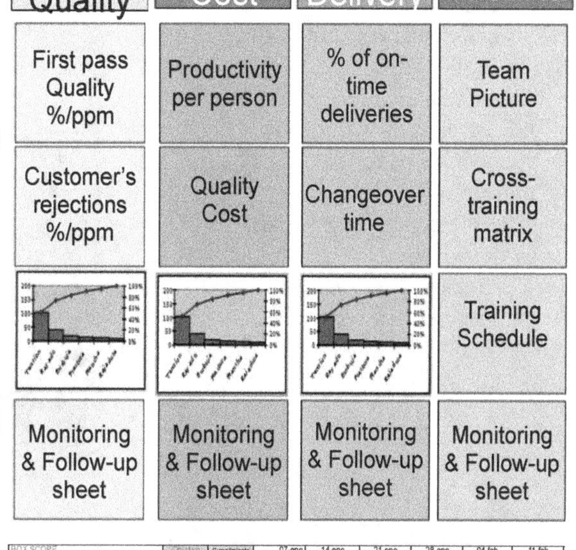

BOX SCORE	Objetivo	Cumplimiento	07-ene	14-ene	21-ene	28-ene	04-feb	11-feb
Unidades por persona	21		14.00	16.00	18.00	20.00	19.00	23.00
Envíos a tiempo	100%		100%	100%	100%	100%	100%	100%
Tiempo de entrega (días)	4		3	4	1	3	4	5
Días de puerta a puerta	3		6	12	23	14	9	7
Calidad a la primera	95%		80%	80%	80%	85%	85%	85%
Nivel sigma	5		4.10	4.30	4.11	4.32	4.70	4.34
Costo de no calidad	$ 250		$ 2,345	$ 3,112	$ 645	$ 345	$ 1,245	$ 3,124
Costo promedio del producto	$ 300		$ 343	$ 337	$ 362	$ 338	$ 337	$ 325
Valor del inventario	$ 545,000		$ 3,004,234	$ 2,334,756	$ 2,945,893	$ 2,564,382	$ 1,945,678	$ 1,234,975
Vueltas de inventario	12		4.50	4.00	6.70	7.10	8.30	9.00
Costo de mantenimiento	$ 500		$ 2,820	$ 645	$ 2,323	$ 976	$ 1,733	$ 758
Evaluación 5's	100%		100%	100%	100%	100%	100%	100%
OEE	85%		70%	73%	75%	79%	81%	81%
Tiempo de lanzamiento NP	25 días		42	42	42	42	37	37
Velocidad de demanda			3.45					
Velocidad de producción			5.50					
Capacidad Disponible								
Ingreso			$ 432,050	$ 384,870	$ 422,456	$ 389,754	$ 389,465	$ 466,032
Costo de Material			$ 189,000	$ 125,879	$ 167,453	$ 133,456	$ 133,234	$ 197,034
Costo de Conversión			$ 131,200	$ 130,242	$ 132,000	$ 132,426	$ 128,034	$ 111,342
Utilidad Bruta del Value Stream			$ 111,850	$ 128,949	$ 123,003	$ 123,872	$ 128,197	$ 147,656
Retorno de la cadena			25.89%	33.50%	29.12%	31.78%	32.91%	32.36%

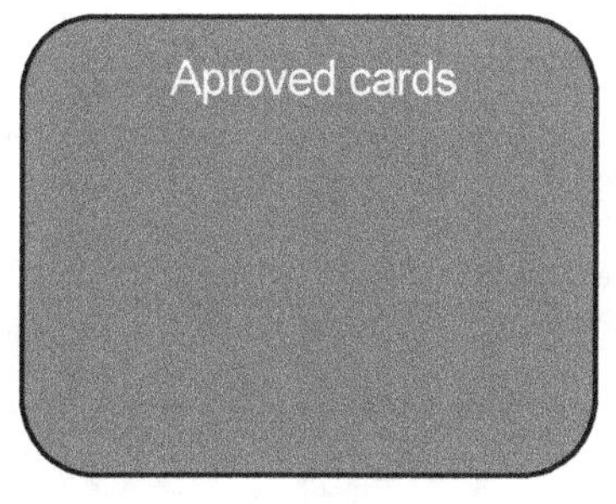

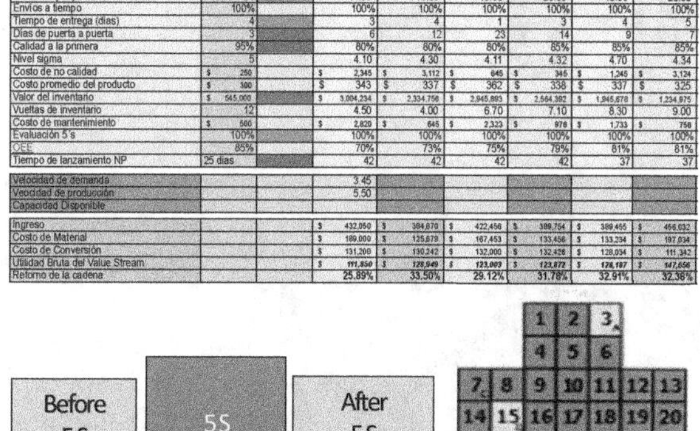

3. Value office design

You must select an area in which the value stream team members will work.

The room must have:
- Visibility to areas that generate value
- A strategic location
- Proper lighting
- Work stations for each member
- A meeting table at the center of the room
- A projector and screen
- Writing board

People responsible for the value stream work full-time in the value office. They have scheduled meetings to review and analyze results, and make decisions.

- Value stream Manager
- Sales
- Planner/Buyer
- Finance
- Process Engineer
- Quality Engineer
- Equipment Engineer

LSSI
LEAN SIX SIGMA INSTITUTE

4. Analyze the performance of the value stream

A. Update the Box Score

The **Box Score** provides:

- Lean measurements that replace traditional ones

- Methods to identify the financial impact of Lean improvements

- An improved way to understand the cost of products and the cost of value streams

- New ways to make decisions related to price and profitability

- Better ways to decide between buying or producing

- A way to focus the business around the value created by customers

BOX SCORE	Objective	Progress	7-Jan	14-Jan	21-Jan	28-Jan	4-Feb	11-Feb
Units/person	21		14	16	18	20	19	23
On-time deliveries	100%		100%	100%	100%	100%	100%	100%
Lead time (days)	4		3	4	1	3	4	5
Days from door-to-door	3		6	12	23	14	9	7
First pass yield	95%		80%	80%	80%	85%	85%	85%
Sigma level	5		4.10	4.30	4.11	4.32	4.70	4.34
No quality cost	$ 250		$ 2,345.00	$ 3,112.00	$ 645.00	$ 345.00	$ 1,245.00	$ 3,124.00
Average product cost	$ 300		$ 343.00	$ 337.00	$ 362.00	$ 338.00	$ 337.00	$ 325.00
Inventory value	$ 545,000		$ 3,004.23	$ 2,334.76	$ 2,945.89	$ 2,564.39	$ 1,945.68	$ 1,234.98
Inventory turns	12		4.5	4	6.7	7.1	8.3	9
Maintenance cost	$ 500		$ 2,820.00	$ 645.00	$ 2,323.00	$ 976.00	$ 1,733.00	$ 756.00
5S evaluation	100%		100%	100%	100%	100%	100%	100%
OEE	85%		70%	73%	75%	79%	81%	81%
Launch time (days)	25		42	42	42	42	37	37

Demand			100					
Production capacity			200					
Available capacity			50%					

Revenue			$ 432,050	$ 384,870	$ 422,456	$ 389,754	$ 389,455	$ 456,032
Material cost			$ 189,000	$ 125,679	$ 167,453	$ 133,456	$ 133,234	$ 197,034
Conversion cost			$ 131,200	$ 130,242	$ 132,000	$ 132,426	$ 128,034	$ 111,342
Value Stream Net Profit			$ 111,850	$ 128,949	$ 123,003	$ 123,872	$ 128,187	$ 147,650
Return			25.89%	33.50%	29.12%	31.78%	32.91%	32.38%

- Every week the **box score** is updated to identify opportunities and to know if the established goals have been reached.

- The **box score** meeting is held every week with all members of the value stream.

B. Value stream cost analysis

Traditional cost method

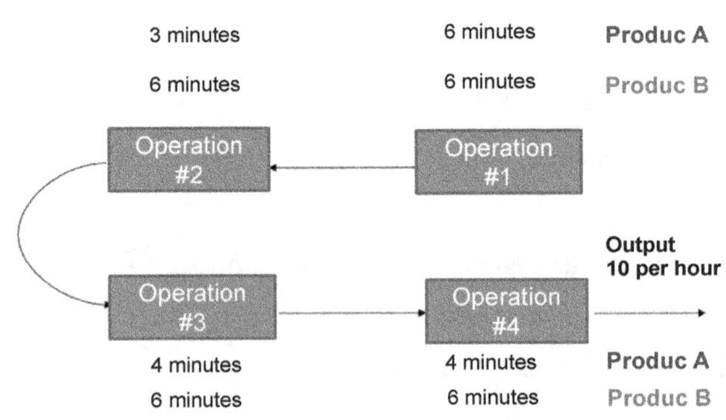

Product / Service A

Labor   = 17 minutes
Labor rate: $24.23 per hour
Overhead rate: 600%

Labor   = $6.87
Overhead = $41.19
Material = $42
Total Cost = $90.06

Product / Service B

Labor   = 24 minutes
Labor rate: $24.23 per hour
Overhead rate: 600%

Labor   = $9.69
Overhead = $58.15
Material = $42
Total Cost = $109.84

Lean Accounting

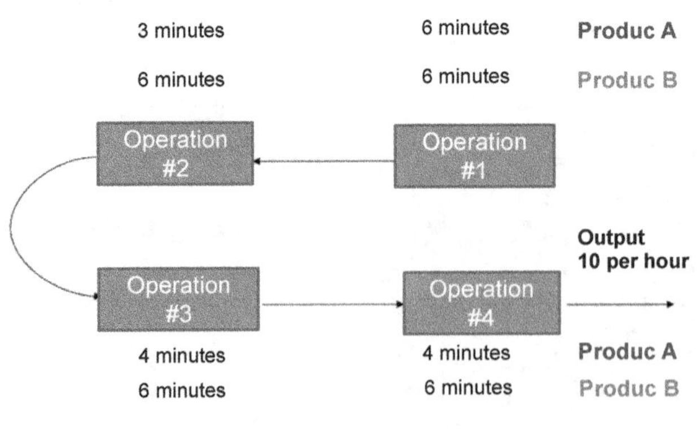

Product / Service A

Conversion cost = $580 per hour
Units produced = 10 per hour

Per unit
Conversion cost = $58
Material Cost = $42
Total Cost = $100 (REAL COST)

Product / Service B

Conversion cost = $580 per hour
Units produced = 10 per hour

Per unit
Conversion cost = $58
Material Cost = $42
Total Cost = $100 (REAL COST)

LSSI
LEAN SIX SIGMA INSTITUTE

Lean Accounting benefits

- Eliminate waste from administrative and accounting processes
- Internal understanding of the real costs of a company's products and/or services
- Better marketing and sales strategies
- Members of the value stream share a common objective
- Guides decision-making in relation to the value created for customers and the business
- Financial statements delivered every week
- Eliminate bureaucracy that prevents better communication and therefore better results
- Calculate and evaluate the benefits of a Lean implementation

5. Design how level 3 (management team) will work, if the pilot was successful in the deployment phase

Level 3 responsibilities

▸ **Managers, directors, and chief executives**

- Strategic planning and monitoring
- Monthly review of results and annual strategic planning
- If necessary, weekly meetings for decision making
- Look for new business opportunities
- Solve level 3 problems
- Support level 2
- Conduct "Gemba Walks" frequently

Balanced Scorecard

Guidelines	Objectives	Goal	(YTD)	
Financial	Economic Value Added	4%		
	ROI	12%		
	RONA	18%		
	$ Backlog	$100,000		
	Throughput	$4,010,000		
	Cash Flow	$800,000		
Commercial	Profit / Loss	$2,060,000		
	Revenue	$5,000,000		
	Net Promoter Score	78%		
	Market Share	22%		
Processes	Conversion Costs	$1,250,000		
	Direct Cost	$990,000		
	Inventory Value	$650,000		
	Total Investment	$27,364,000		
People	Internal NPS	90%		
	Employee engagement	90%		
	Turnover	1%		
	Talent Development	85%		

LSSI — LEAN SIX SIGMA INSTITUTE

	January	February	March	April	May

Example: initial situation

Individual work centers

The ACME company had a departmental work structure and separate offices in which people only worked in groups when they met in the meeting room.

Departmental structure

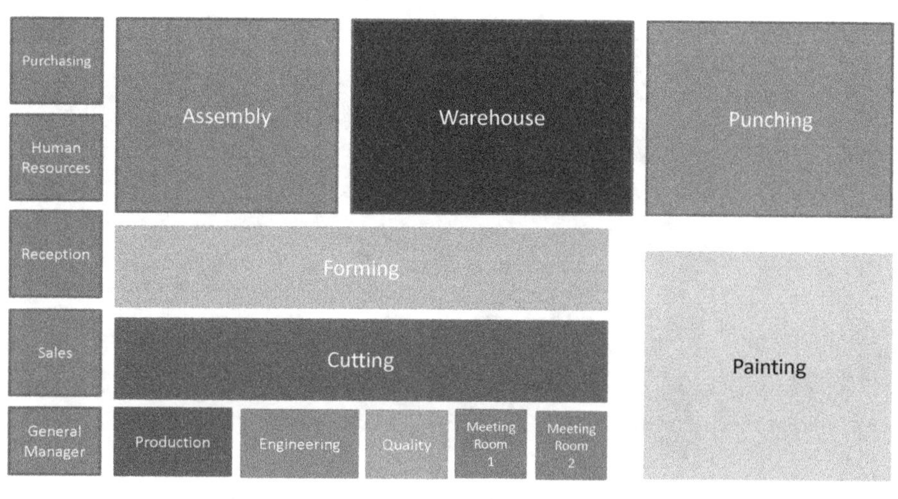

Define the pilot value stream

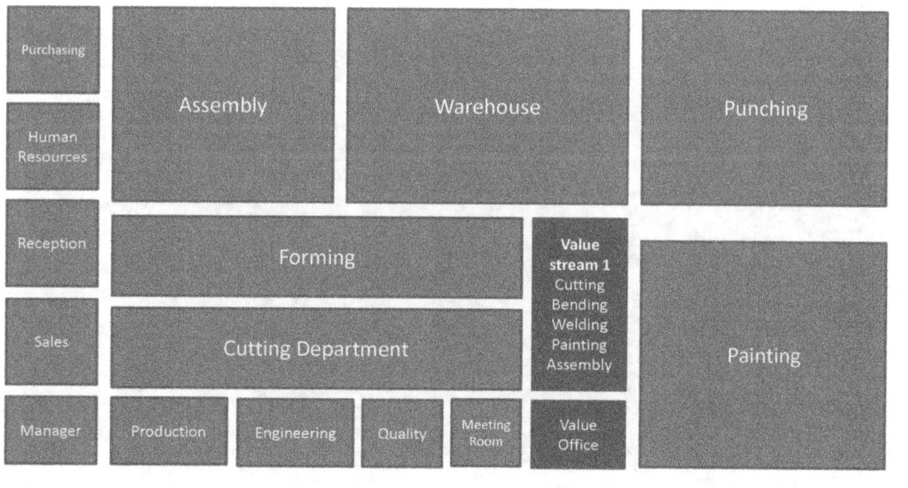

Members:
Value Stream Manager
Equipment Engineer
Materials Engineer
Process Engineer
Coach
Cost Engineer
Planner-Buyer

Deployment of all value streams

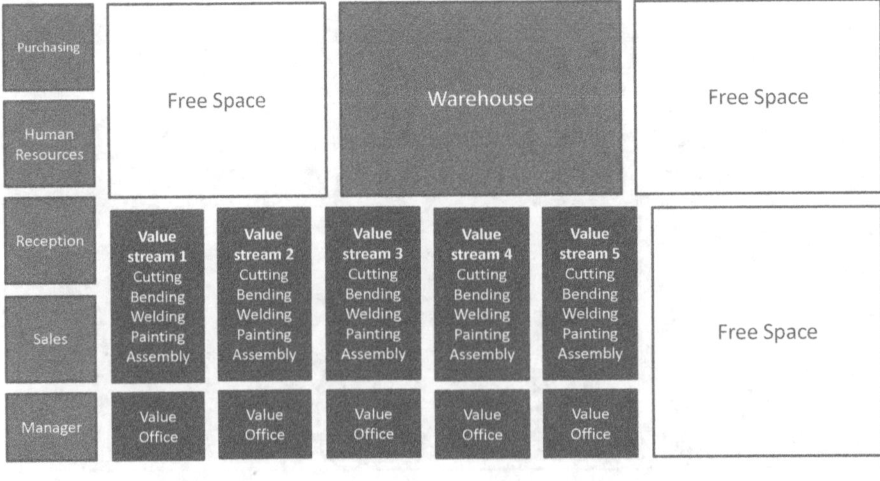

LSSI LEAN SIX SIGMA INSTITUTE

Talent Development

Learning objectives

1. Understand the importance of talent development in an organization.
2. Understand the process to implement talent development as a competitive advantage.
3. Apply a creative and effective method to transfer knowledge.

Content

> Introduction
> Background
> What is talent development?
> Key elements
> When should an organization implement it?
> Talent development procedure
> Benefits
> Exercise

- Many issues in **quality**, **communication**, and **productivity** are not caused by a lack of technology or special resources.

- What is really needed is sufficient time dedicated to **teaching**, **learning**, and **practicing**.

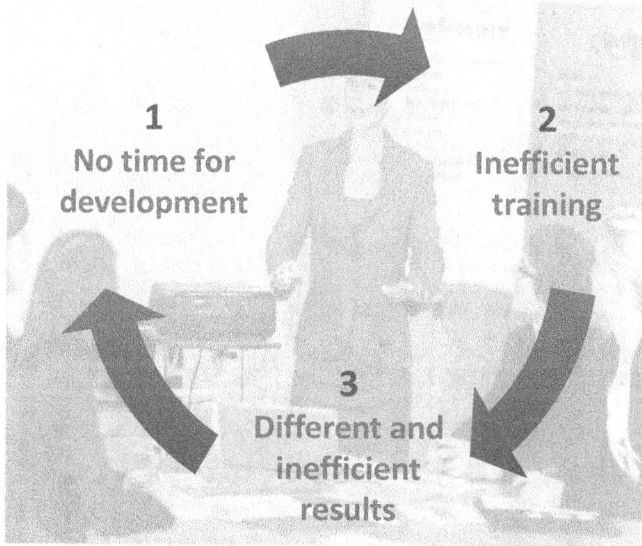

Background

- When the United States entered WWII, they began to deploy young working men to the war. However, the country still had to produce day-to-day products required by the country and its people.

- The new labor force was made up of older men and women, who were not necessarily prepared to take over those jobs.

- The US government decided to develop the **Training Within Industry (TWI)** method to train the employees who would be replacing the workers going to war.

- The program would prepare trainers in any industry who are capable of teaching employees key skills, in order to help them perform their jobs effectively (i.e., leadership skills, teaching skills, improvement skills, etc.)

- The program was aimed for: managers, supervisors and team leaders.

- The training program included 3 courses:
    - Job Instruction (JI)
    - Job Methods (JM)
    - Job Relations (JR)

TWI: A forgotten program

- At the end of World War II, the United States stopped the TWI program.

- The teaching system is not encouraged or promoted among U.S companies.

Toyota brings it back

- Toyota reinvented the TWI program.

- Toyota produces cars and also talented people.

- Processes are designed to be analyzed and taught by leaders, who will then challenge the system continuously.

What is talent development?

- Talent development is a methodology used to develop a learning culture by **attracting, training, and retaining employees**.

- It includes accompanying each person on their journey to help them reach their full potential.

Key elements

TWI Components

Charles Allen 4-step Learning Process	TWI			PDCA Cycle	Scientific Method
	Job Instructions	**Job Methods**	**Job Relations**		
Preparation	Prepare the Worker	Breakdown the job	Get the facts	**Plan** - Observe data and reality; decide on a problem; define it	Observation & Description
Presentation	Present the Operation	Question every detail	Weigh & decide	**Do** - Analyze the problem; propose a countermeasure	Formulation of an hypothesis
Application	Try Out Performance	Develop new method	Take action	**Check** - Try the countermeasure; check the results	Use the hypothesis to make predictions
Testing	Follow Up	Apply new method	Check results	**Act** - If successful, standardize the change; if not, start the cycle over	Test the predictions through experiments

LSSI
LEAN SIX SIGMA INSTITUTE

Talent Development

- As soon as an organization is established

- Any time where lack of knowledge is generating problems. Example: quality, speed, cost, sales, etc.

Talent development procedure

1. Prepare the organization to develop exceptional people.

2. Identify critical knowledge.

3. Transfer knowledge to others.

4. Verify the learning process and success of the program.

1. Prepare the organization

Assess the needs

- Develop the strategy (Hoshin Kanri) to focus on critical knowledge

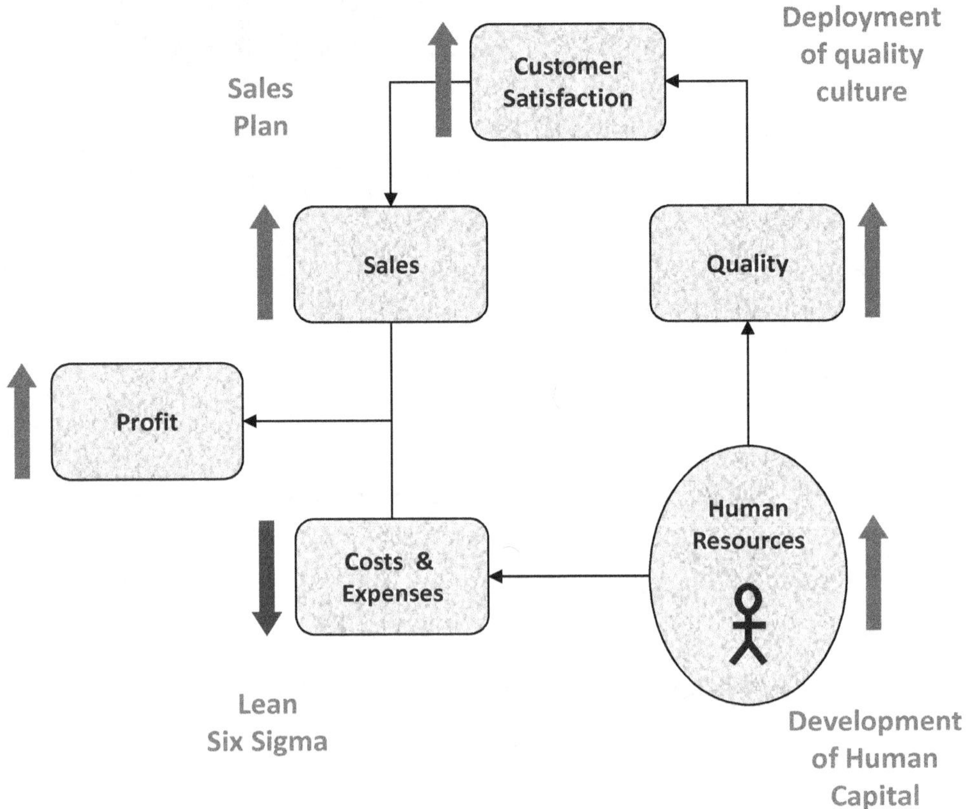

LSSI
LEAN SIX SIGMA INSTITUTE

- According with box score results, define where training is required

- Results determine the areas of focus for Talent Development

BOX SCORE	Objective	13-May	20-May	27-May	3-Jun	10-Jun	17-Jun
Units per person	21	14.00	16.00	18.00	20.00	19.00	23.00
On-time deliveries	100%	100%	100%	100%	100%	100%	100%
Lead time (days)	4	3	4	1	3	4	5
Days from door to door	3	6	12	23	14	9	7
First pass quality	95%	80%	80%	80%	85%	85%	85%
Sigma level	5	4.10	4.30	4.11	4.32	4.70	4.34
Quality costs	$ 250	$ 1,125	$ 2,320	$ 645	$ 345	$ 1,245	$ 3,124
Average product cost	$ 300	$ 343	$ 337	$ 362	$ 338	$ 337	$ 325
Inventory value	$ 545,000	$ 3,004,234	$ 2,334,756	$ 2,945,893	$ 2,564,392	$ 1,945,678	$ 1,234,975
Inventory turns	12	4.50	4.00	6.70	7.10	8.30	9.00
Maintenance costs	$ 500	$ 2,820	$ 645	$ 2,323	$ 976	$ 1,733	$ 756
5S Evaluation	100%	100%	100%	100%	100%	100%	100%
OEE	85%	70%	73%	75%	79%	81%	81%
Demand		500	600.00	550.00	495.00	620.00	545.00
Production Capacity		650	650.00	650.00	650.00	650.00	650.00
Available capacity		23%	8%	15%	24%	5%	16%
Revenue		$ 432,050	$ 384,870	$ 422,456	$ 389,754	$ 389,455	$ 456,032
Material Costs		$ 189,000	$ 125,679	$ 167,453	$ 133,456	$ 133,234	$ 197,034
Conversion Costs		$ 131,200	$ 130,242	$ 132,000	$ 132,426	$ 128,034	$ 111,342
Value Stream Profit		$ 111,850	$ 128,949	$ 123,003	$ 123,872	$ 128,187	$ 147,656
Value Stream ROS		25.89%	33.50%	29.12%	31.78%	32.91%	32.38%

2. Identify critical knowledge

Break down the job into steps for teaching

Only 20% of knowledge is critical and contributes 80% of the results.

Critical

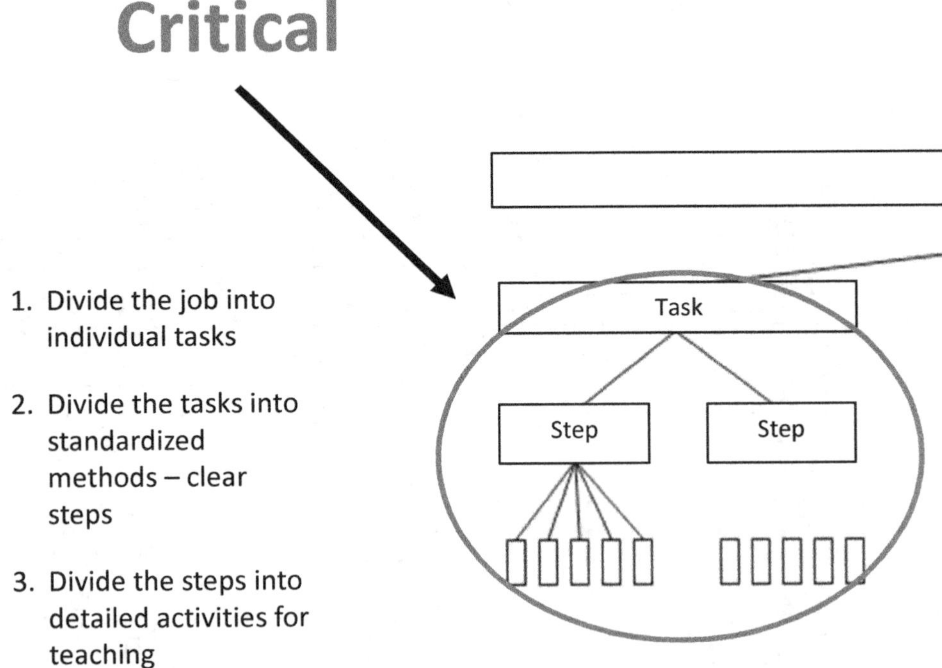

1. Divide the job into individual tasks

2. Divide the tasks into standardized methods – clear steps

3. Divide the steps into detailed activities for teaching

LSSI
LEAN SIX SIGMA INSTITUTE

Job breakdown includes three main parts:

1. Identify key steps in the work task
2. Identify important information within the steps (key points)
3. Why are the key points important?

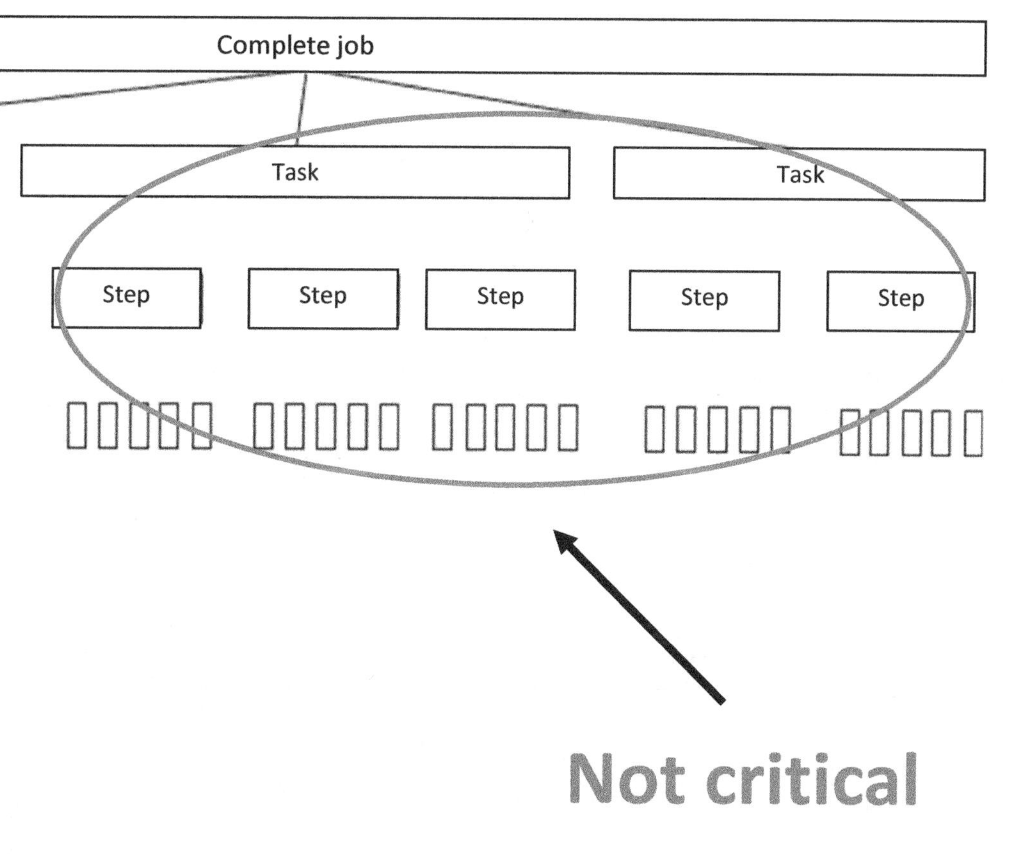

Identify critical knowledge

Critical knowledge must be documented in a work instructic

APOLLO SPRAYERS - WORK INSTRUCTIONS	
Area: Subassembly	Item: T100 Cord

KEY STEPS	KEY POINTS **Safety** **Quality** **Technique** **Time**
Step # 1 Insert strain relief	1. Insert thinner Edge first
	2. Strain relief must be 13" from the start of the cord
Step # 2 Peel wire terminals	1. Make sure no cooper wire is showing on the inside of the connector
Step # 3 Crimp wire terminals	1. Twist wires before crimping
	2. Make sure to crimp connectors with the inside of the crimping tool
	3. Make sure no cooper wire is showing on the inside of the connector
Step # 4 Check if wire terminals are loose	1. If yes, back to step 3

LSSI
LEAN SIX SIGMA INSTITUTE

Team leader	
Supervisor	
Created by	Rodrigo Diaz
Date	3/20/2012

REASON FOR KEY POINTS

Righ dimension to fit T100 and reach the switch

Could lead to problems during testing and final assembly

3. Transfer the knowledge

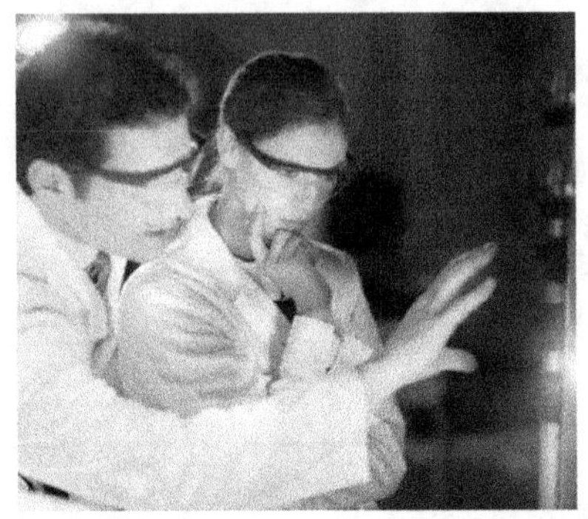

Present the Operation

Job Instruction

Prepare the Worker

Present the Operation

Try Out Performance

Follow Up

Step 1: Trainer performs the task (without speaking).

Step 2: Trainer mentions the steps as he/she performs the task.

Step 3: Trainer mentions the steps, as well as the key points, as he/she performs the task.

Step 4: Trainer mentions the steps and key points and explains why the key points are important, as he/she performs the task.

LSSI
LEAN SIX SIGMA INSTITUTE

4. Verify the learning process and success of the program

- Continuous monitoring and review of tasks

- Guide the student towards independence

- The team leader trains each member of the team

- Success is shown through results, not only actions

"For the things we have to learn before we can do them, we learn by doing them." Aristoteles

Evaluate knowledge and performance

Multi-skills Matrix

Each task has to be learned at the highest level of detail and must be evaluated according to the skills shown during practice.

Name	Register	Get info.	Diagnose	Fix	Testing	Invoice	Check out	Total	Ranking
John Smith	1	3	4	0	2	1	1	12	C
Bob Hope	5	5	5	5	5	5	5	35	G
Robert Mills	3	4	2	1	5	4	2	21	E
Dave Jones	1	0	4	4	2	2	1	14	C

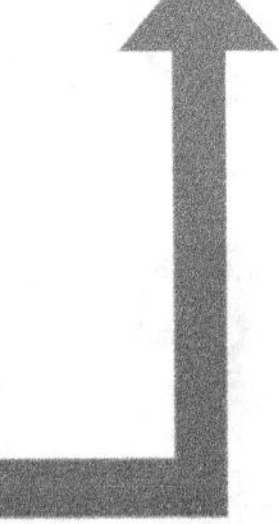

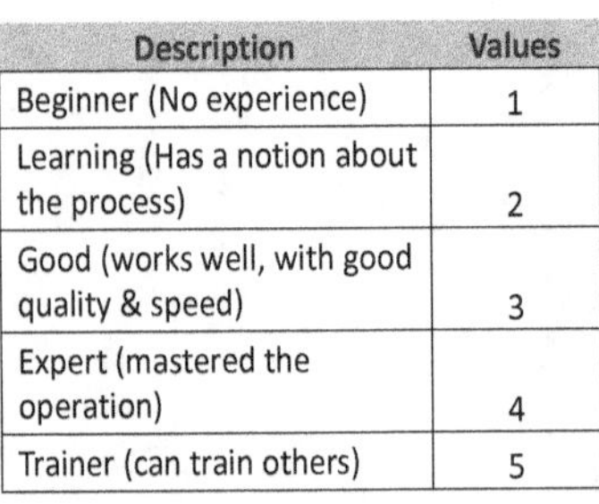

Description	Values
Beginner (No experience)	1
Learning (Has a notion about the process)	2
Good (works well, with good quality & speed)	3
Expert (mastered the operation)	4
Trainer (can train others)	5

Ranking	Point Range	Salary
A	1 to 5 points	$ 750
B	6 to 10 points	$ 890
C	11 to 15 points	$ 990
D	16 ato20 points	$ 1,025
E	21 to 25 points	$ 1,290
F	26 to 30 points	$ 1,440
G	31 to 35 points	$ 2,000

LSSI — LEAN SIX SIGMA INSTITUTE

Benefits

- A more stable workforce

- Reduces accidents

- Documented knowledge of critical processes

- People who are willing and motivated to learn

- People who are willing and motivated to teach

- Creates quality excellence

- Greater job satisfaction

- Minimal costs arising from poor quality

- High employee retention rates

Companies that have implemented TWI have reported improvements of at least 25% in their productivity.

- Establish the critical processes in your organization
- Choose one of them
- Identify critical knowledge
- Document the process in a work instruction format
- Prepare a trainer
- Teach the operation using the 4 steps method
- Evaluate knowledge and performance and discuss the benefits

LSSI
LEAN SIX SIGMA INSTITUTE

**Sales and operations planning.
S&OP in 14 steps**

Cristina Peña Andrés

**Lean Manufacturing.
Step by step**

Luis Socconini

**Lean Six Sigma.
Management System
for Leaders**

Luis Socconini, Carlo Reato

Substance Abuse Treatment

Ana Adan, Conrad Vilanou

**Practical guide to the
Incoterms 2020 rules**

David Soler

**Shipping & Commercial Case
Law**

Albert Badia

Lean Six Sigma Management. Certification Manual

Luis Socconini

Lean Six Sigma White Belt. Certification Manual

Luis Socconini

Lean Six Sigma Yellow Belt. Certification Manual

Luis Socconini

Lean Six Sigma Green Belt. Certification Manual

Luis Socconini

Lean Six Sigma Black Belt. Certification Manual

Luis Socconini

Lean Services. Certification Manual

Luis Socconini

València, 558 – 08026 Barcelona – Tel. +34-931 429 486 – marge@margebooks.com – www.margebooks.com

www.ingramcontent.com/pod-product-compliance
Lightning Source LLC
LaVergne TN
LVHW080433200726
843507LV00004B/804